A Kid's Guide to Tabletop RPGs

T0384229

A Kid's Guide to Tabletop RPGs

EXPLORING DICE, GAME SYSTEMS, ROLEPLAYING, AND MORE!

Written by **GABRIEL HICKS**

Illustrated by **DAVE PERILLO**

RP|KIDS
PHILADELPHIA

Running Press Kids
Hachette Book Group
1290 Avenue of the Americas, New York, NY 10104
www.runningpress.com/rpkids
@RP_Kids

Distributed in the United Kingdom by Little, Brown Book Group UK,
Carmelite House, 50 Victoria Embankment, London, EC4Y 0DZ

Printed in China

First Edition: June 2023

Published by Running Press Kids, an imprint of Perseus Books, LLC,
a subsidiary of Hachette Book Group, Inc. The Running Press Kids name
and logo are trademarks of the Hachette Book Group.

The Hachette Speakers Bureau provides a wide range of authors for speaking events.
To find out more, go to www.hachettespeakersbureau.com
or email HachetteSpeakers@hbgusa.com.

Running Press books may be purchased in bulk for business, educational, or promotional use.
For more information, please contact your local bookseller or the Hachette Book Group
Special Markets Department at Special.Markets@hbgusa.com.

The publisher is not responsible for websites (or their content)
that are not owned by the publisher.

Print book cover design by Mary Boyer
Print book interior design by Frances J. Soo Ping Chow.

Library of Congress Cataloging-in-Publication Data has been applied for.

ISBNs: 978-0-7624-8109-5 (paperback), 978-0-7624-8110-1 (ebook)

1010

10 9 8 7 6 5 4 3 2 1

Contents

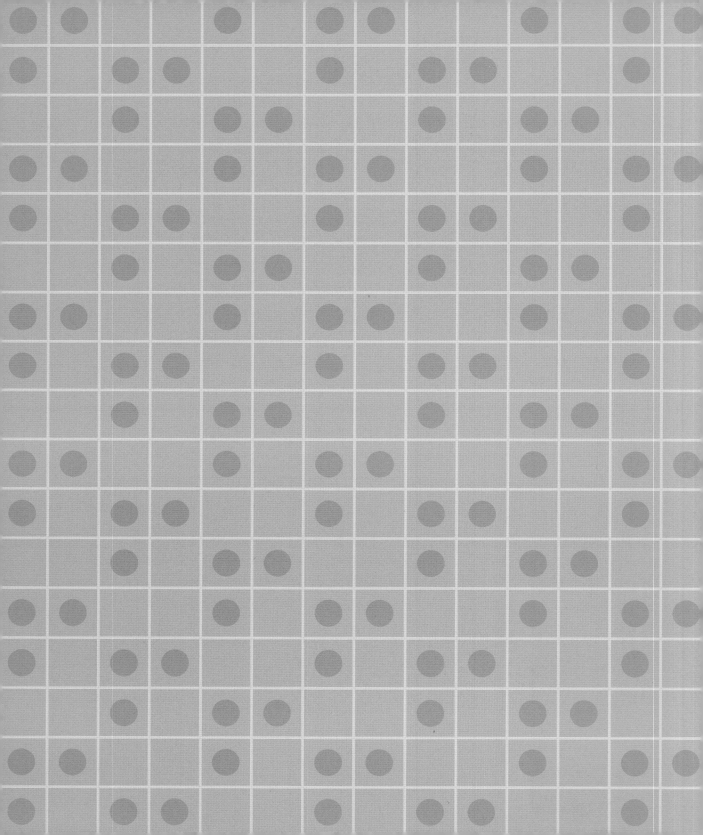

What Is a Tabletop RPG?

TABLETOP ROLEPLAYING GAMES (OR TTRPGS for short) can be so many different things. They are ways to explore worlds, they are storytelling tools, they are interactive experiences, and, to put it simply, they are games. Some of the most popular and common ones are Dungeons & Dragons, Pathfinder, and Fallout, just to name a few, but there are hundreds of games from major publishers as well as independent designers. Some are designed around exploring magic and fantasy worlds, and others are focused on science fiction or space travel; there are even games focused on everyday experiences that give you a chance to step into someone else's shoes. TTRPGs give people a chance to live a different life and experience, to tell a story they might not have been able to before. I got into tabletop RPGs when I was in college, but my imagination and desire to be a hero and play in these stories started when I was way younger. I grew up watching the *Star Trek* television series and *The Lord of the Rings* cinematic trilogy, a bunch of different worlds that made me want to play *in* them and make my own stories. So I started writing books about fighting dragons and ogres with groups of heroes wielding magic weapons and riding mystical beasts. I originally thought I could only interact with these worlds as a writer or reader, but discovering tabletop roleplaying games really emphasized how wrong I was (in the best way).

There are so many ways to describe what TTRPGs are, and even I can describe only so much. However, this book will be your gateway to the world of tabletop RPGs and give you the basics about what it means to play a tabletop roleplaying game, what it means to run a session for one, and even what it means to make one because, yes, you can make one. Anyone can make a game; it takes creativity and hard work, but you can do it.

May the dice be ever in your favor,
GABRIEL HICKS

TABLETOP RPG GAMES YOU MIGHT KNOW

Dungeons & Dragons ✳ Pathfinder ✳ Magic: The Gathering ✳ Settlers of Catan ✳ Root ✳ Monopoly ✳ Disney Villainous ✳ Bananagrams

CHAPTER ONE

Getting Equipped for Adventure

BEFORE WE BEGIN, LET'S GET the vocabulary and equipment you will need to navigate the world of tabletop roleplaying games! This chapter will explain some of the rules and tools to help you get started telling amazing stories. We'll get into how to tell those stories in later chapters! If you're going on an adventure, you'll need to be prepared for what type of adventure it is—you wouldn't want to go camping without proper supplies. (I wouldn't at least; you might be cooler than I am.) So, to help get you equipped, we're going to learn about **dice**, your **table**, the roles of the **narrator** and the **party**, and **character sheets**!

Dice

Let's start with dice. Dice in tabletop roleplaying games have varied shapes, sizes, and sides and are called polyhedral dice. Dice are so common that it's probably harder to find tabletop games that don't use dice than it is to find those that do. There are six basic types that are used in all the variations of tabletop games, but the most common is the six-sided die. You have probably used this die in board games like Yahtzee or Clue, but there are many other kinds you can use when playing tabletop games. Some games will involve all or a bunch of variable kinds of dice; others will have you use only one kind.

The distinct die types are named and recognized by how many sides they have. The most common ones you'll use for gaming are the four-sided, six-sided, eight-sided, ten-sided, twelve-sided, and twenty-sided dice. Though something you will notice is that they're usually called by a slightly different name, which is the letter D and the number of sides. For example, instead of saying "a four-sided die," you would say, "a D4." Then an eight-sided die is a D8 and a twenty-sided die is a D20! There are ten-sided dice, D10, that have digits in the tens, so they count for ten, twenty, thirty, and so on.

There's a history to the different types of polyhedral dice. The D6 is one of the oldest dice to exist. Historians have traced its use back to before 5000 BCE in a prehistoric game referred to as knucklebones. These dice were often made from wood, bones, and even clay. The D4 can be traced back to the royal game of Ur (also known as the "game of twenty squares") from ancient Mesopotamia and were responsible for telling players where to move their pieces across the board. Both the D12 and D20 can be traced to Egypt, Greece, and Rome. Twelve- and twenty-sided dice from Egypt with letters of the Greek alphabet on each face have been found.

HISTORY CHECK!

QUIZ

Guess the Die by Shape

A
B
C
D
E
F
G

Die Shape Answer Key

A. D12
B. D6
C. D10
D. D10
E. D8
F. D4
G. D20

The Table

Adventuring parties come in all shapes and sizes. Many games have an average of four to six players, with one being the narrator, and these are the people who make up your "table." Think about your favorite TV shows, movies, or video games where you have a group of adventurers all traveling and working together. They go on perilous journeys, fighting dragons, delving into dungeons, and maybe even trying to retrieve a lost gem that belongs to their dragon parent. You'd be surprised by the kind of stories people will tell, but they are fun! Your table is made up of the people playing those characters and the rules and guidelines that are established for that story with your special group. The storyteller, the party, you're all part of the same table, and you work together to have the most fun you can.

Speak with a parent or older family member who can be your go-to "game guardian." Your trusted adult should be there so if something goes wrong or you need someone to help, you can rely on them. They will help resolve any conflict so you can play the game together in the way you enjoy the most.

So you might be wondering, "Is there an ideal table size?" The good news is that the answer will change for everyone. Your table might change based on the game you're playing, the story you want to tell, or even how you are feeling that day. If your two favorite people in the world are hanging out with you at your place, and you are happy to spend time playing a game together, then a table of three can be ideal!

The Narrator

Many TTRPGs need someone to narrate and guide their players (also known as the party, see section below) through the story. The story could be one they made up, or they could be following an adventure that was written by someone else (we'll talk more about writing games on page 91).

This role is often referred to as the dungeon master (DM), game master (GM), storyteller, or lore keeper, but there are plenty of other cool titles. If you're feeling creative, you can even make up your own name with your group for this role at your table! In this book I mainly refer to them as the narrator.

Along with telling the story, a narrator also is often responsible for controlling additional characters for the party to interact with. These characters are called non-player characters, or NPCs. NPCs might be creatures, monsters, merchants, villains, or random townsfolk who, for some reason, like to challenge players to dance battles. This is your world, after all. NPCs are also known as non-party characters because they aren't directly controlled by a member of the central party. This way the acronym, NPC, stays the same, but it helps the narrator, who is playing a bunch of characters instead of a main character in the party, feel like a player too.

The Party

Everyone else at the table listens and reacts to elements of the story as a player character, or PC. Many people in the community also call them party characters because they are members of the direct party and the focus of the main story. Characters created by the party are usually the main characters, the heroes of the story. As a party member you are playing in this story and world with everyone else at the table. You'll come up with your own backstory and create your character—most likely using a character sheet—and you'll discover how your character is related to everyone else in the party. Do you and another party member want to make characters who are siblings, family members, or even married? What about best friends or enemies? Talk it through with the other people in your party, so when you're playing in this world, everyone has an idea of what will be happening to start with.

Using the terms "party characters" and "non-party characters" at your table helps remind everyone that the narrator is just as important and as much of a player as everyone in the main party. When you're playing tabletop RPG games, remember that you are all playing and creating the story *together*.

Character Sheets

Another thing you'll hear about when you are getting ready to play a tabletop RPG is a character sheet. While almost every game's character sheet is different, they all serve as a place to keep track of all the information about your PC. That information includes their name, how old they are, their abilities and skills, and even some extra-interesting background information, like they really enjoy pickles or they have a dog named Leopold.

Since they are sheets for characters, even NPCs sometimes have them too! If you're the kind of narrator who likes to keep notes about all the details and backgrounds of your non-party characters, then these sheets are perfect for you. Not only will they help you keep track of who is who when you are telling your story, but you can also write down how the party met that character or even secret information the character might have to help the party on their journey. See page 115 for a sample Character Sheet.

Now you've got your equipment, so let's head out into adventure!

ROLL FOR INITIATIVE

So, how can you play tabletop RPGs? Well, the two main ways are either playing in person or digitally. Many groups meet in person and share a physical table, while others use websites like Roll20, D&D Beyond, or Foundry to connect with their friends. These sites allow people to take all the tools they have at their physical table and share them in a digital space.

First, you'll want to discuss with your friends whether having in-person or digital game night is better—or you can always do both! In person means you'll get to share a fun table and have those moments where you simply just give someone a look. There's nothing like a group of friends sitting together and being able to laugh with them right next to you. The value of a digital game means being able to play with anyone around the world! It's one thing to play with people in your neighborhood, but it's a whole different experience when you have friends in different states together. Remember that everyone has different schedules and responsibilities, so it is important to be flexible. You might decide to play in person, getting together for a specific gaming night, or maybe you are going to decide to have a weekly game or a game every other week, or maybe you all just play once a month. As long as you are thoughtful and include everyone in the decision, there is no wrong answer.

Next, be sure that all members of the group check in with their family about hosting or attending a game night. If you are playing digitally, ask your guardian to help you set up your account and make sure that you are playing with the correct people.

Don't forget to check your school, local library, or game shop to see whether there are any gaming clubs you can attend after school. If not, it could be a great opportunity for you to start one and meet new friends.

INSIGHT CHECK!

Game designer and author of this book, Gabe Hicks, shares his memory of his very first character. You will read more about Gabe as you go through this book and discover other Insight Checks!

• • • •

GABE: I played a fancy sorcerer! A character who had magic, but their magic is something they were born with and they got even better with it over time. I think the story was that his magic came from a dragon that gave him the gift when he was a baby for some reason and then he developed this magic as he grew up. His name was Cross. He was an elf, and he loved sweets, if I remember right. He eventually got dragon scales on his body and stuff because he was getting that much stronger. It was really cool.

CHAPTER TWO

A Vast Sea of Games

THERE ARE AN INFINITE VARIETY of worlds for you to explore in the tabletop gaming space, and new ones are being made literally every day. There are hundreds of themes and topics for tabletop games from fantasy, science fiction, magical girls, dragons, kids riding bicycles, squirrels, and even bears trying to steal honey. (No, seriously, it's called Honey Heist and it's amazing.)

Games are also made not only for all types of interests but also for all different age groups. There are games made for kids aged ten to fifteen, and games made for kids sixteen and older. Games are like movies in that way! Sometimes the age range is set because of the more mature themes the game explores, and other times it is based on how complicated it gets. Games for younger ages will often be lighter on the rules and setup, but that doesn't mean you won't enjoy them if you're older! This is important to remember when you are deciding what game to play because it can help ensure that everyone has fun and feels comfortable at the table. If you aren't certain if a game is a good fit for you, then ask your guardian to help you.

Because they are basically any game that can be played on a table, there are a bunch of different types of tabletop games out there for you to try out, from board games; to deck-, dice-, or tile-based games; and, of course, roleplaying games. There are even different subtypes in each! There are plenty more types of games, but these are a few examples of each main type of tabletop game.

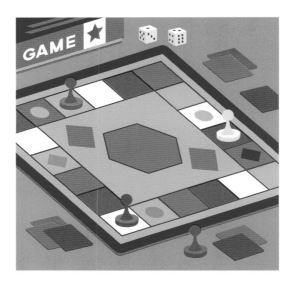

Board Games

Chess, Monopoly, Clue, and Candyland are all examples of tabletop games, and more specifically, board games. There are two main subtypes: games that are great for working together with the group, known as cooperative party games, and games where you play against the other players, known as competitive party games.

Deck-Based Games

These games can either use only a deck of cards, or they can have card decks as a major feature of their gameplay. Apples to Apples and Doomlings are incredible examples of deck-based tabletop games that have players using only decks of cards, while 5-Minute Dungeon and Villainous are games that use cards alongside other pieces. There are also deck-based games with more rules and strategy, called "deck-building" games, where the focus is creating a deck by adding new and different cards to whatever you started with, like Magic: The Gathering or Pokémon, the trading card game.

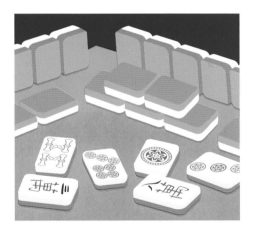

Dice and Tile Games

Some of the most common tabletop games that have been around for the longest time use just dice or tiles. Some common tile games are games like mahjong, dominoes, Scrabble, and even Jenga! Tile games are, you guessed it, games that use tiles as one of their key focuses. This can be building out on the board, placing them in connecting ways, or any other feature but still using the tile as an essential piece. Can you guess the key focus in a dice game? Some common dice games are Cuphead, Yahtzee, and Sagrada, and they are often competitive games.

Roleplaying Games

One of the best-known roleplaying games is Dungeons & Dragons (we'll dig more into the history of D&D in Chapter 3). One of the key elements in a roleplaying game is that the player is asked to create or define the character whose role they're going to take on to experience their story. The difference in general tabletop games versus tabletop roleplaying games is directly in the title, "role." These games are also known as pen-and-paper RPGs—although the term is not as commonly used today because neither a pen nor paper is really necessary.

Generally, the party takes turns describing aloud who their character is and what they're doing in different moments throughout the story. This creative aspect is one of the reasons why some players like playing tabletop RPGs: they get to create a unique character from rules the game provides and pretend (or "roleplay") as if they are truly that character.

Although there's a good number of roleplaying games to choose from, one that stands out is Questlings RPG. This is a roleplaying game designed specifically with younger players in mind, and it has them play "as two characters, one as your kid form and one as the Inner Hero." This is a great game for beginner tabletop roleplaying players and narrators, because it has a storybook and map that provide a framework for roleplaying and building the story to guide you through the game.

Solo Games

These are roleplaying games designed specifically so you can play by yourself. They don't require a narrator or other players because they have mechanics—which are rules that govern and guide the player's actions, as well as the game's response to them—and rules to tell you what happens when you do certain things to guide you through the story. For example, you draw a card from a regular deck (or sometimes special decks like tarot or oracle decks), and the game rules might say that you go left if you draw a diamond card or straight if you draw a club card. The game doesn't require you to make all these choices; it gives you the rules to make the choices for you.

Personally, some of my favorite games are solo games, and if you enjoy reading choose-your-own-adventure books or like playing video games on your own, then these might be a good type of roleplaying game for you to try. In fact, the recent choose-your-own-adventure card games are solo games.

If you ever get a chance, try checking out some solo games, which are games that you can play by yourself or modify to play with other people, and then see what you like about them. One of the best things about a solo game is that you get to be entirely in control of how the story goes. Technically, if you want to change the rules you can, because at the end of the day you are the one playing the game, and your fun is the most important thing.

UNIQUE AND INTERESTING SOLO GAMES TO TRY

Coffee Roaster, by Stronghold Games ✳ Calico, by Alderac Entertainment Group ✳ Colostle, by Nich Angell ✳ The Isle of Cats, by The City of Games ✳ Tiny Towns, by Alderac Entertainment Group

GM-Less Games

Say you want to play a game with your friends but you all want to be players. Well, then you'd want to maybe try a GM-less, or narrator-less, game.

This type of roleplaying game is designed so that you can play it without the need for a single person to be the dungeon master, game master, narrator, or anything of that sort. These games are usually played with a group of people, and technically the game will play itself. Board games are considered GM-less games. However, it is important to remember that there is a difference between a solo and a GM-less game.

The biggest difference between the two types is that you are the player and the narrator in a solo game. However, a GM-less game is designed so that the group and the rules of the game help decide what the story is and what the players will do together, taking turns to fill in the narrator role when needed. A great example of a GM-less game is Wanderhome, in which the group decides their characters and how the story will unfold by working together to each describe little bits of the places they visit and the NPCs they meet.

That said, sometimes a game can be played as a solo or GM-less, so it isn't easy to always say that a game is one or the other. You have the choice with these games to enjoy this narrative adventure on your own or with a group of friends without someone needing to be the storyteller. The game tells you the story as you go along. For example, although the Choose Your Own Adventure card game is technically a solo game, it also includes rules for a voting system and even has additional characters as well as rules for how to divide up who plays which character. No matter what game you end up playing, your table might prefer a GM-less game if everyone wants to build a story equally. There will be days that no one wants to take the role of the narrator, and GM-less games are perfect for those moments and tables!

GM-LESS GAMES TO TRY WITH YOUR FRIENDS AT YOUR NEXT SLEEPOVER OR PARTY

Fiasco, by Bully Pulpit Games ＊ Wanderhome and Sleepaway, by Jay Dragon and Possum Creek Games ＊ Alice Is Missing, by Hunters Entertainment

—— INTERVIEW ——

BANANA CHAN
(SHE/THEY/HE)

Introduce yourself.

> **BANANA CHAN:** Hi! I'm Banana Chan. I'm a game designer; I have worked on a lot of different games, and I publish games through my company. I have also done stuff for Hasbro, Renegade, Wizards of the Coast, and several other companies.

Do you remember how you got started in this industry?

> **BANANA CHAN:** Yes! As a kid growing up, I've always played board games with my dad. We would play Monopoly, Uno, and also a Chinese game that was light in strategy, and I loved them. I didn't get into roleplaying games when I was in high school. I played a game of D&D, and I didn't enjoy myself so I just didn't get back into it. Then years later when I was at college, I went to a convention and started getting back into board games, and I also ended up getting into LARPing (live-action roleplaying).
>
> I had so much fun with both of those that I started wanting to make my own stories and decided I wanted to start designing tabletop games. It was hard, because, especially when you're younger, it just felt harder to understand that you need a good group to play with, ya know? You're being vulnerable when you're playing sometimes, and that requires some trust, so I wanted to make that happen in the games I made.

What is it like making games for a younger generation?

BANANA CHAN: It's hard to tell, right, because the games I've been making, specifically like Questlings RPG, one of the most important details was to make it as accessible as possible. We wanted to keep in mind it isn't just the kids playing but also the parents running the game for the kids. What if a parent has never run a game or it's an older kid who has never roleplayed before? I found that a lot of tabletop roleplaying games can be intimidating because there's not a step-by-step guide. You read the handbook and then just sort of do it. There's die rolls and a lot involved, but it's not step by step. When we designed Questlings we wanted to make sure it had a guide. You could read through it like a storybook, and there were prompts to answer, and the things you knew how to do you were told specifically. That was our biggest goal! We wanted it to be accessible and make it so players knew what to do as they were playing through the game.

Do you have any advice for narrators who also want to make games?

BANANA CHAN: For getting over performance anxiety, definitely one of the things that I tell myself is that this is my game and I know what's going to happen and I know what to do. If players have feedback, then listen to them because they're saying it for a reason. Also, be open to telling your players that you need stuff too because you're also a player. You aren't only doing this for other people, you're also doing this to have fun. Having that understanding and setting those expectations is incredibly important.

It's hard, especially if you're starting to GM or you've been a GM for a while, because whenever you play with a new group there's different play cultures to be aware of. Different groups play differently. Honestly, playtesting has helped me adapt. It sometimes involves talking to strangers or new people and having to get an idea. A quick Session 0 helps, explaining the rules clearly, making sure everyone is treating each other with respect and not overstepping boundaries. That can be just as hard to do with a group you don't know well as it would be with friends. I struggle with that even now because I get along with my friends but sometimes I don't know what it's going to be like at the game table, and that's okay. If we all communicate properly, that's one of the biggest things that will make everyone happier.

Do you have any advice for people who want to be GM/DM/narrators who haven't done it before?

BANANA CHAN: Yeah! Definitely try to take it easy when it comes to running the game. Be forgiving and be gentle with yourself. Don't push yourself too hard, either. It is okay to make mistakes, and you can keep going unless someone at your table asks you to stop and wants to try something else. Try not to put too much pressure on yourself creating these stories because, ultimately, you're there to play with these other people, and hopefully everyone else is too, and they should be respectful of your time and energy.

CHAPTER THREE

Dungeons, Dice, Dragons, and Danger

"**YOU ENTER THE DUNGEON OF** Smokehouse the silver-scaled dragon. You and your party smell smoke in the air, but something else on top of it. . . . It's pie!"

Originally published in 1974, Dungeons & Dragons was not only the first commercial TTRPG but also one of the most popular roleplaying games even today. Created by designers Gary Gygax and Dave Arneson, the game is now designed and produced by a company in Renton, Washington, called Wizards of the Coast, or WotC for short.

It has been more than forty-five years since Dungeons & Dragons was published, and it has gone through so many different versions—it is currently in its fifth edition, also called 5e.

OSR, or "old school renaissance," games are new TTRPGs that are inspired by the earlier editions of D&D and the games that came out in the '70s and '80s. One of the interesting features of OSR games is that they ask the players and narrator to fully embrace the story and try unique and clever solutions when faced with a tricky situation or combat. The narrator also doesn't rely as much on a standard rule book and instead has more control over the challenges and combat. They act as both a storyteller *and* a referee, deciding the outcomes of players' actions, based on whether they think it is possible and fits with the story instead of just on the roll of the die.

In the world of D&D, you get to pick your character's origin, making a character that is completely customized to what you like and who you want to be, whether that is an elf or a human or even a vampire. You then pick their class, which is kind of like their job. Is your character a wizard who really likes dragons, a barbarian who was raised in the mountains, or a druid who comes from the forest and is a protector of a magic lake? The primary classes available in Dungeons & Dragons 5e are the artificer, barbarian, bard, cleric, druid, fighter, monk, paladin, ranger, rogue, sorcerer, warlock, and wizard.

SOME CLASSY
CHARACTERS

ARTIFICER

Masters of invention, artificers use ingenuity and magic to unlock extraordinary capabilities in objects. They see magic as a complex system waiting to be decoded. They will then harness it in their spells and inventions. Their tools channel their arcane power to create not only new equipment but new life. The magic of artificers is tied to their tools and their talents, and few other characters can produce the right tool for a job as well as an artificer.

BARBARIAN

For some, their rage springs from a communion with fierce animal spirits. Others draw from a roiling reservoir of anger at a world full of pain. For every barbarian, rage is a power that fuels not just a battle frenzy but also uncanny reflexes, resilience, and feats of strength.

BARD

Whether scholar, skald (a composer and reciter of poems honoring heroes), or scoundrel, a bard weaves magic through words and music to inspire allies, demoralize foes, manipulate minds, create illusions, and even heal wounds. The bard is a master of song, speech, and the magic they contain.

CLERIC

Clerics are intermediaries between the mortal world and the distant planes of the gods. As varied as the gods they serve, clerics strive to embody the handiwork of their deities. No ordinary priest, a cleric is imbued with divine magic.

DRUID

Whether calling on the elemental forces of nature or emulating the creatures of the animal world, druids are an embodiment of nature's resilience, cunning, and fury. They claim no mastery over nature but see themselves as extensions of nature's indomitable will.

FIGHTER

Fighters share an unparalleled mastery with weapons and armor and a thorough knowledge of the skills of combat. They are well acquainted with death, both meting it out and staring it defiantly in the face.

MONK

Monks are united in their ability to magically harness the energy that flows in their bodies. Whether channeled as a striking display of combat prowess or a subtler focus of defensive ability and speed, this energy infuses all that a monk does.

PALADIN

Whether sworn before a god's altar and the witness of a priest, in a sacred glade before nature spirits and fey beings, or in a moment of desperation and grief with the dead as the only witness, a paladin's oath is a powerful bond.

RANGER

Far from the bustle of cities and towns, past the hedges that shelter the most distant farms from the terrors of the wild, amid the densely packed trees of trackless forests, and across wide and empty plains, rangers keep their unending watch.

ROGUE

Rogues rely on skill, stealth, and their foes' vulnerabilities to get the upper hand in any situation. They have a knack for finding the solution to just about any problem, demonstrating a resourcefulness and versatility that is the cornerstone of any successful adventuring party.

SORCERER

Sorcerers carry a magical birthright conferred upon them by an exotic bloodline, some otherworldly influence, or exposure to unknown cosmic forces. No one chooses sorcery; the power chooses the sorcerer.

WARLOCK

Warlocks are seekers of the knowledge that lies hidden in the fabric of the multiverse. Through pacts made with mysterious beings of supernatural power, warlocks gain magical effects both subtle and spectacular.

WIZARD

Wizards are supreme magic users, defined and united as a class by the spells they cast. Drawing on the subtle weave of magic that permeates the cosmos, wizards cast spells of explosive fire, arcing lightning, subtle deception, brute-force mind control, and much more.

These descriptions come directly from the the game Dungeons & Dragons. You can find these descriptions and more information on D&D Beyond with a guardian's supervision.

Once you decide on your origin and class, you get to start building out who your character is going to be—how strong they are, how wise they are, how charming they are—by following the game's rules and guidelines.

Not only is being able to create your character one of the super-fun parts of playing D&D, but it is hard to imagine what other tabletop RPGs would be like without this game. Dungeons & Dragons helped show other people how to create and play in this new space, and the world of tabletop RPGs has only continued to grow and get more creative since the '70s.

HISTORY CHECK!

The term "dungeon master," or DM, comes from, you guessed it, Dungeons & Dragons. Of course, just because they are in the title of the game doesn't mean that your adventure needs to actually take place in a dungeon or even have dragons. (But let's face it, dragons are cool, so why not have one?) In retrospect, "dragon master" would have also been a really cool name. Honestly though, you can use whatever name you want for the role of the narrator!

Speaking of expanding worlds, an important aspect of tabletop games, especially roleplaying games, is the ability to add and build off different parts of the game so that there is always new and interesting stuff for players and DMs to work with. The makers of Dungeons & Dragons are big believers in that, and, over a single year, they can put out anywhere from five to ten new core rule books that help expand the world. Sometimes the books include new places to explore, new classes to play, or new items to use—most of the time, a combination of all three.

MORE DUNGEONS & DRAGONS ADVENTURES TO EXPLORE

If you're looking for a fancy magic academy, there's Strixhaven: A Curriculum of Chaos, which introduces the fantastical setting of Strixhaven University. This world is drawn from the multiverse of Magic: The Gathering and provides rules for creating characters who are students in one of its five colleges. Characters can explore the setting over the course of four adventures, which can be played together or on their own. Each adventure describes an academic year filled with scholarly pursuits, campus shenanigans, exciting friendships, hidden dangers, and perhaps even romance.

Up next is Fizban's Treasury of Dragons, which has all the dragons you could ask for. Dragon slayers and dragon scholars alike can harness the power of dragon magic and create unique and memorable draconic characters, as well as dragon-themed encounters, adventures, and campaigns.

Are you always looking for something new in your adventures? Then try Journeys Through the Radiant Citadel. This book features a collection of thirteen short, stand-alone adventures with challenges for character levels 1–14. Each adventure has ties to the Radiant Citadel, a magical city with connections to lands rich with excitement and danger, and it can be run as a one-shot (read more about these on page 97) or as part of your ongoing campaign.

New Horizons

D&D might have been the game to help start the tabletop roleplaying game space and community, but there are countless other games to try, both big and small! If you are looking for a game with a specific theme or genre, here are some great ones to check out and play at your table. And don't worry—if you can't find what you are looking for, then maybe it is time for you to make your own TTRPG (which I'll talk more about in Chapter 7).

You might be seeking mystery and want to act like Robin Hood in a fancy steampunk world, then maybe you should try Blades in the Dark, a game where you and a crew of others try to pull off a heist as a group. Or maybe your table wants something that is more of a fantasy experience from D&D: then Quest might be the game for you. In this game, you build your character sheet by asking unique roleplaying questions. Rather than just focusing on mechanics, you explain what you want your character to do and decide together with the game master how to make it happen in the game. This is a great mechanic (and game) for beginners to experience the world of TTRPGs at their own pace. Some other great genres and TTRPGs to try are these:

FANTASY

- **THE DRAGON PRINCE RPG:** Based on the popular TV show *The Dragon Prince*, you and your table can explore the world of Xadia.
- **KIDS ON BROOMS:** Grab your wand and step into a world of magic, mystery, and danger as a witch or wizard at magical school in this narrative-first TTRPG.
- **HERO KIDS:** A fun Dungeons & Dragons–style game, perfect for playing with younger family members and for trying out your skills as a narrator.
- **STARSWORN:** Part choose-your-own-adventure, part storytelling game that starts at a fair where stars fall and bring the world powerful magic. Perfect for playing with younger family members.

SCIENCE FICTION

- **COYOTE & CROW:** Created by an all-Native team, this game envisions a world where Indigenous nations weren't colonized and instead grew into advanced, diverse civilizations that recently survived a massive climate disaster.
- **LASERS & FEELINGS:** Explore the uncharted regions of space in this game with members of your crew while you wait for your captain to recover from contact with a strange psychic entity.
- **BEAM SABER:** Built off Forged in the Dark, this is a game about the pilots of powerful machines.
- **TALES FROM THE LOOP:** Play as local teens dealing with everyday troubles while solving mysteries, from strange machines to weird creatures, created by a particle accelerator, known by the locals as the Loop.

SUPERPOWERS

- **GLITTER HEARTS:** An action-packed game you play as everyday people who transform into powerful magical heroes to fight off the forces of evil.
- **MASKS: A NEW GENERATION:** A superhero game where a team of young heroes fights villains and saves lives as you struggle with everyday troubles like discovering who you are and falling in love.
- **MUTANTS & MASTERMINDS:** Built on a modified version of the D20 system (which is what D&D uses), this game allows you to create any hero or villain you desire and have unique adventures.

MODERN

- **KIDS ON BIKES:** Play as a ragtag group of everyday kids solving mysteries that involve strange, dangerous, and powerful forces in your small town.
- **BUBBLEGUMSHOE:** A game where you play as teen sleuths finding clues and solving mysteries in your hometown.
- **MALL KIDS:** A playful, collaborative story-based game about a group of teens who work together at a mall and the events that make up your lives.

Of course, these are only a handful of examples, but if there's a theme or style of play that you are looking for in your next game, chances are there's a TTRPG out there for you.

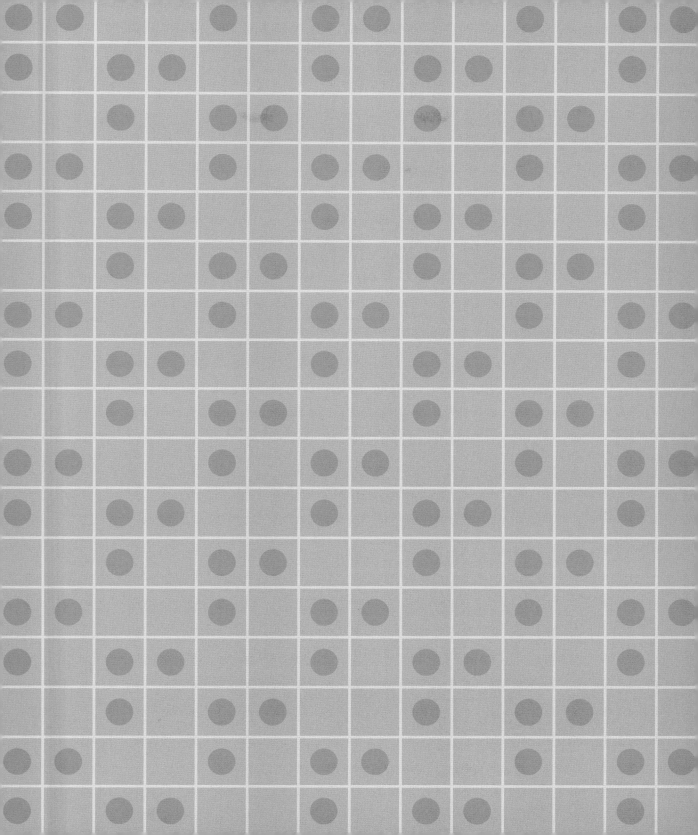

CHAPTER FOUR

Being a Narrator and Building a Party

DUNGEON MASTER, GAME MASTER, DRAGON master, narrator, or storyteller—no matter what name you choose to go by—is an important role in tabletop RPGs. You are creative, weaving a cool story and acting out as different non-party characters and big, bad, evil guys and gals (BBEGs). You lead by taking charge of the game's rules and also helping set up days and times for your group to come play with you. And you are caring, making sure that everyone at your table is having a good time.

There's a lot involved in being the narrator, but don't let it overwhelm you. Here are a few guidelines to always keep in mind:

- Be creative, flexible, and always make sure to have fun.
- It is okay to make mistakes.
- It is okay to talk out things with your party.
- Find ways to make bad dice rolls as fun as good ones—it makes the story more interesting.
- You are playing this game with everyone, not against them.
- You can always ask an older family member for help.

There are a lot of different ways to be the best narrator you can be. There are even books and articles and stories that can help you find tips and tricks you can use at your own table. That said, before you get started, always remember the first guideline: be creative, be flexible, and make sure to have fun.

Your game should be enjoyable for you and everyone who is joining you at the table. Sometimes this isn't as easy as it sounds. During the game, you may come up with ideas that are fun for you that might be really unfair or take away from everyone else's enjoyment, so you might have to change your ideas a bit. This is where being creative and flexible comes in. Maybe one of your players interprets one of your ideas differently and it isn't going the way you want, or maybe they interact with the idea in a way that makes the game less fun by accident. That's okay! This might be a great time to slow down and talk to your players about what is going on and see if the group can come up with a creative solution. And if talking it out with the group isn't working or if someone is feeling uncomfortable, then it is also okay to have your guardian step in to help.

Being a narrator is a lot of responsibility and a good deal of work, but it is also really rewarding, as long as you remember these guidelines. Don't forget that tabletop RPGs are about going on adventures and having a good time with your friends and family!

INSIGHT CHECK!

Do you prefer being a party member or the narrator? Is one easier than the other for you?

GABE: That's a hard question, but I don't have a preference as a whole. I might have a preference during the day or something though.

Some days I love being the storyteller. I love getting to put together a world and playing in it together with people. I get to see the ideas I've had come together and how players overcome my creative challenges. It's really satisfying sometimes, but it's also scary because I have been doing this for years and I never stop worrying that maybe it's not going to be perfect. I might forget something and that's hard. It's always worth it, it is worth it every time, but I still get nervous. I don't get nervous as a member of the party.

I usually just trust that the narrator is going to help guide me and everyone else into something fun and interesting. The only backstory I really have to focus on is my own, and I can focus more on helping to add to the story and collaborate with the story rather than leading the story more when I'm a party member, so that's why I was saying it kind of just depends on the day.

I do like both, and I like the option of having both, which is sometimes why I end up playing multiple games a week. Right now, as I'm writing this, there are three games that I'm in during the week—I am the narrator for two of them and I am a party member/player in the other one. That variety definitely helps me and makes it easier for me to feel like I'm getting a nice balance.

Picking a Game

Okay, so the first thing that you are going to want to decide is who is going to be at your table. That means thinking about which friends and family are interested in playing the same kind of games that you are. So, do you want to find a group that's all excited about riding fantasy dragons? Do you want to play with a group that is really into gardening? Do you want a party that isn't so focused on fighting monsters and would rather explore a mystery?

It is okay to want to play a specific type of game and with a group that is eager to play it too. It is also important to be open minded and thoughtful about who is in your group. If it is your first time narrating or playing a specific game, then maybe it would be better to have your best friends and some family at your table until you get more comfortable. Other times, you might find that best friends don't want to play that kind of game or aren't available, so maybe you'll have to see if friends from your school or your neighborhood might be interested in playing.

Think of it this way: You want to play a game about horses, but if your best friend really doesn't like horses, then would they have a good time playing this game with you? You might love the idea of getting to spend time with them doing something you enjoy, but if they don't like horses, well, then, it's not going to be enjoyable for them, and that is going to make playing the game less fun for everyone. However, if your next-door neighbor loves horses, then they might be extra excited to play a game about them.

If you find a club or even if you end up starting one for tabletop games, hopefully this book will help you get playing soon!

PICKING A GAME
FLOWCHARTS

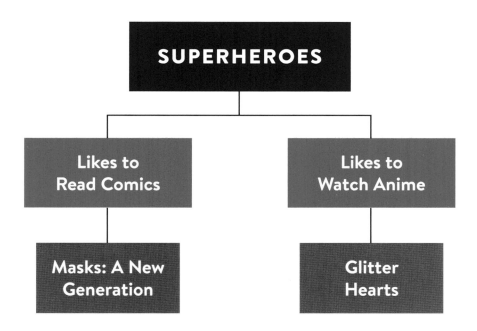

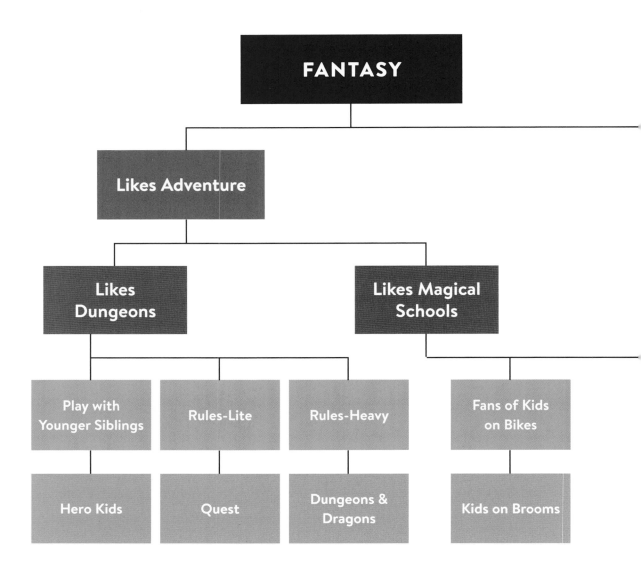

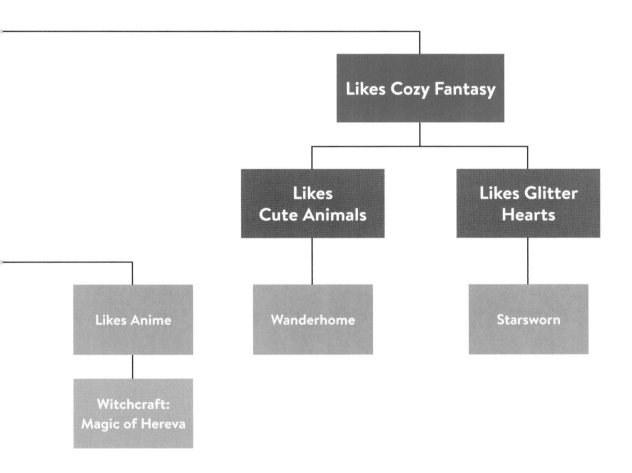

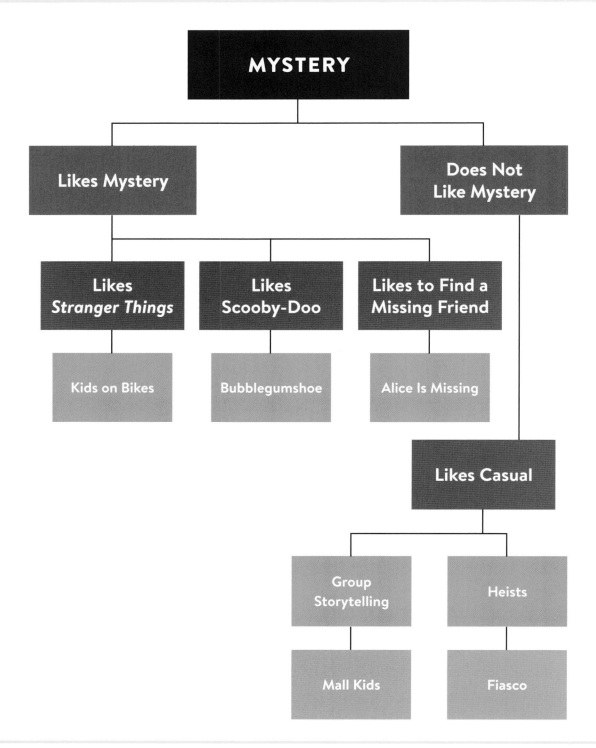

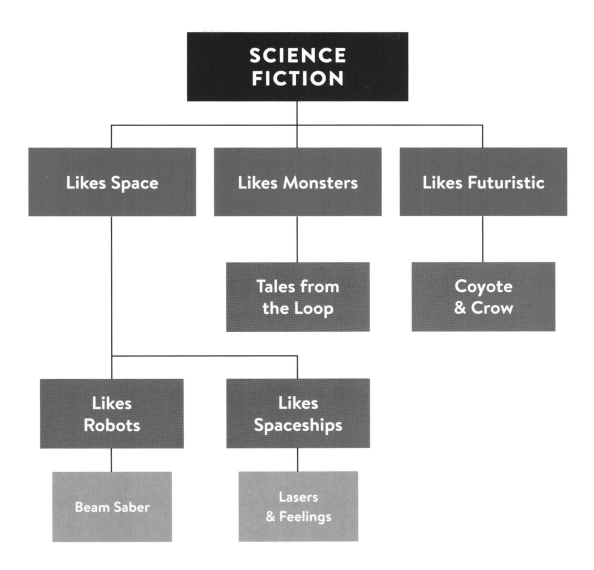

Gathering Your Adventurers

There's still a very important issue that matters when you're putting together your adventuring party, and that's making sure you are being inclusive. Inclusion is incredibly important in your games. This can mean a whole bunch of different things: playing with more people, especially people who don't necessarily look like you or have your same experiences. Different experiences are part of what makes us all human and also part of what makes each of us such good storytellers. A story I make up out of my experience will be different from yours, and that's exciting! Opening up your table to people who aren't just like you means making them feel welcome, and you'll get new ideas and adventures from it.

Games are for everyone, no matter what you look like or sound like or talk like or how or where you grew up. Two people who have lived entirely different lives can still love the same types of games. Everyone deserves to have fun, and taking that chance away means missing out on all the good adventures you could have gone on together.

When you go to school or walk around, there are so many people who look different from you. That means that when we're playing in games it makes sense to have that same diversity in these worlds. When people are different from you that means you learn something different from them, which is fun. If everyone was the same, how boring with that be? Imagine being in a world where everyone can talk to animals, but people only talk to birds. Birds will probably have some fun and weird things to say, but what do you think the cats would say? What about the different types of birds that see everything from up high or that fly at super-fast speeds? Then there are even the dolphins and fish that see everything from underwater, and you would just never hear about it. When you have more and different ideas, views, and perspectives in your games, you get a lot more to explore, and we all want to be explorers in some way.

Consider asking someone you don't know to join you. It's a great way to welcome a new kid in class. You might be strangers at first, but I'd say fighting a dragon together is a great way to make a new best friend. Look into starting a club (with supervision from an adult) if there's not already one around. Invite someone you might not know very well but you think would be fun to adventure with. You might know what all of your best friends will do, but not what a new friend will do. And they might do something even more interesting than you could have ever imagined.

Telling a Good Story

The party finally reaches the enormous castle. You look up to the sky and see a strange figure who looks like a skeleton made of blue bones staring down at you. They start to laugh and cackle, which is strange because it's a skeleton, so it doesn't have, like, vocal cords, but it's super spooky and weird. Now the gate in front of all of you opens outward. Inside, there is a courtyard, and you see a huge figure who looks to be half man, half bull. They're flexing their arm muscles before they begin to brush their foot against the ground one time, two times, three times . . . before sprinting toward you. Roll initiative.

When you are the narrator, you are responsible for setting up a scene. You describe a whole bunch of details so your players can imagine their characters existing in the space. Don't forget to include what something smells like, what it looks like, what it sounds like, what it feels like, and even sometimes what it tastes like. You are helping to paint a picture that is in your head so that your players can see it too, but there is an endless canvas for you to work with.

A good question to ask yourself is, What do you want this game to be like? Think about the setting and the tone of the game you want to play. Is it happy and full of jokes, or is it more serious? Is there a lot of action, or is the action split up to give the table space to roleplay more? Start putting these ideas together, and then ask your table what they think or might want to try, so you can combine that with your ideas and create something everyone will enjoy!

INSIGHT CHECK!

TTRPG DM and crafter extraordinaire Vee talks about how taking inspiration from her writing background makes her a stronger narrator. You can read more about Vee in her interview on page 82.

· · · ·

VEE: I have learned the nuances of what goes into building a story. So, especially as a DM, I have learned that I'm comfortable with plotting everything out because of my writing and creative background. A plotline is where you use bullet points to highlight the details, and then you build a campaign and a story with the players from that list of bullet points. Then I have some other techniques I can fall back on as a writer and as a reader to help flesh the story out or provide fun twists to the bullets as we go along. It is definitely something that is fun to try when you're the DM!

YOUR WORLD, YOUR STORY

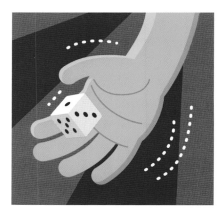

Alright, let's grab a six-sided die, something to write with, and something to write on. Below are a bundle of charts with six options to help you start a unique story. First, fill out Chart 5: Surprise! with six surprising or unusual things that could happen. Next, roll your D6 for each chart, and see what you get! Then, write out a scene with all your chosen answers as if you were the narrator at your table. If you like what you have, then you should use it during your next game! Don't forget you can always make more charts and new answers to keep things interesting.

CHART 1: WHO
SOMEONE OR SOMETHING THAT IS A KEY PART OF YOUR STORY

1. A strange, cloaked figure who likes to rhyme when they speak
2. A friendly talking animal
3. A bearded man with a deep voice who wears red sunglasses
4. A piece of jewelry that can talk
5. A living statue
6. A dragon transformed into a person

CHART 2: WHAT
SOMETHING HAPPENING WITH THE WHO IN THE SCENE

1. Is asking for help with retrieving an item they lost
2. Has been trapped somewhere and is calling for help to get out
3. Wants to sell someone a special item they've been holding onto for a long time
4. Has a mystery they need solved
5. Is looking for the way to the nearest town
6. Is challenging someone to a contest

CHART 3: WHERE
THE LOCATION OF YOUR SCENE

1. In a tall forest with wind blowing through the trees
2. In the throne room of a castle
3. In the marketplace of a busy city
4. Underground in a deep cave
5. Near a large lake with ripples on the surface
6. In an inn where food and drinks are being served

CHART 4: WHEN
THE TIME OR SEASON WHEN YOUR SCENE IS TAKING PLACE

1. A dark and stormy night
2. A warm spring day
3. A cold day during a snowstorm
4. An early morning
5. Dinnertime
6. A nice, crisp fall day

CHART 5: SURPRISE!
SOMETHING QUIRKY AND UNUSUAL THAT APPEARS OR HAPPENS IN YOUR SCENE

1. _____

2. _____

3. _____

4. _____

5. _____

6. _____

Respecting the Table

You probably have an idea of what sort of game you want to play now, and it's important to find the adventuring party that you'll be happy to play those kinds of adventures with! Even if you're not the narrator, you are just as important as a member of the party. There are a bunch of ways you can be the best player possible and help everyone at your table. There are even tools you can use to have a safer, more enjoyable time (we'll learn more about safety tools in Chapter 5). They exist so that if there's a problem, you have an agreed-upon way to solve it or avoid even getting into any issues.

First is to be patient, especially if someone (maybe even you) is new to a game. Your story-teller might be learning the rules, or the game, or the themes, and rushing someone might make it even scarier. Being patient at the table gives everyone the time they need to learn and get more comfortable with the game, plus it means that they are way more likely to be patient with you!

Second, your character doesn't have to be perfect. You get to decide what'll make them fun to play, but they don't have to be the best at everything. Sometimes being bad at things helps to balance out a story. Your character doesn't have to be the "best" at something for them to be fun to play trying to do something.

Third, share the spotlight. You might have a really good idea, but if you share that idea or pull another party member into the moment, you might just make their day! Sharing the spotlight and the excitement means that more people can make the excitement even bigger! Your table will have ideas you never thought of and help to make good ideas even greater!

Finally, don't forget that at the end of the day, it is just a game! You might want to argue if something didn't go the way it says in the rules, and you should talk it out if there are problems, but this is a game. Being "right" isn't always what the table wants to do. The storyteller might have different ideas for how the story or game works than the rules say. It helps to spell it out ahead of time, but if they didn't it's okay to talk about it! It's okay to set your own rules for your own games! Setting house rules, even if they're different from the printed ones, doesn't mean you're playing wrong if everyone agrees and wants to play with those rules. You're the ones playing, and you should play in a way that everyone enjoys, even if those rules deviate from the printed ones in the game.

It's not okay to sit at the table and argue about how someone is playing wrong or running the game wrong. If things get too heated and it's hard to process, ask your guardian to step in and help resolve conflict within the group. They are there to help and make sure you can have a good time, so please rely on them when things get too hard.

If this kind of argument keeps coming up, it might just not be the table for you, and that's okay! Cooperation and compromise should go hand in hand, and when they do you'll have a way more fun time. If you remember these four things, and you can do them with your adventuring party, then you have probably found a group of adventurers to tell amazing stories with. Good luck, adventurers! I'm rooting for you.

JEN KRETCHMER
(SHE/THEY)

Introduce yourself.

JEN: Hi, I am Jen Kretchmer, I am an actor, and I am a producer for TV and for table-top goodies and streaming stuff. I am a streamer. I play on a number of different streamed tabletop games. I am an author for D&D's Candlekeep Mysteries and have written for Starfinder. I created the accessibility and gaming resource guide, as well as the disabled pros and tabletop directory. I worked on the game Haunted West. I am a disability consultant for a number of different brands and properties including Skybound games. Specifically, I work a lot on The Walking Dead and also The Adventure Zone. Just a bunch of fun different things.

Do you remember how you started playing tabletop roleplaying games?

JEN: Vividly! So, my first encounter with tabletop roleplaying games was at summer camp. My brother was playing D&D with a number of friends of mine, and everybody was really into it, and so he tried to get me into it. He's younger than I am, and he was trying to explain it to me because I loved fantasy and I loved science fiction. I was completely primed for it, but there was just something about it that wasn't connecting with me. Then fast-forward about three years and I was hanging out with a bunch of my friends in my senior year of high school. We're talking about playing D&D, a couple of them had never played before, some of them had, and one of them said, "Hey, I will DM a campaign. Let's play D&D."

So, I went and I asked my brother if I could borrow his books. And I have never given them back—they're on my bookshelf right next to me. I started playing with the second edition, and that game went on for many years, and that was the beginning of the end.

Can you tell me about your first character?

JEN: Yes, I can. Her name was Aoife, and she was a half-elf druid. I think I was really timid in terms of developing her character because I was still figuring everything out. What the system was, what I was allowed to do and what I wasn't, but I know that her go-to combo in the second edition was Entangle, Fireball, and she had a hawk as well, I believe.

What was your first time DMing like?

JEN: So, I had created this idyllic little town, and I had spent months preparing and writing up all the places and creating a handout that was the town's pamphlet, like a welcome guide for visitors kind of pamphlet, that I gave my players. And I had a playlist for every single location they might go, and I expected them to just sort of meander into the city, but instead they sprinted in and they said, "We needed to talk to the mayor," and, naturally, the mayor was the one person I hadn't created and they were like:

PLAYER: We need the council and I'm going to the council!

JEN: What council? There's no council! I didn't make it.

PLAYER: There's no council Oh, gosh.

JEN: The council is away on a spa retreat four days away!

And so immediately, right off the bat, I did not know what I was doing.

And actually a thing that I'm simultaneously proud of and not proud of was that I stepped out of the game for a second, and I said, "Look folks, I did not prepare for this. I was not anticipating that this is where we were coming from. So, I need you to just bear with me on the town council thing and kind of go with some of the hooks that I'm prepared for," and we worked it out and had fun.

But yeah, it was terrifying, but the nice thing is that was my first session and the very first thing that happened to me as a DM, so right off the bat I knew this is what being a DM is. Sometimes it means never knowing what the players are going to do and always knowing that they will stray from the path that you planned for them and any possible path you have imagined.

Do you still get scared when it comes to DMing?

JEN: Every time, constantly. Same with streaming, I get nervous every time. I think it's much more self-imposed because I don't think my players are disappointed. Instead, it's my fear that my players will be disappointed that I am not giving them the experience that they want. I know that there have been times that I have apologized after games for not having run a good session, and the players are like, "What are you talking about, that was awesome!"

Ultimately, that doesn't matter because there is no perfect. There is no exactly right way to do things in a game. You know, not every game is going to be equally fun, and not every session is going to be equally spectacular, because if they all are spectacular, then how do you know when you have a truly great game? So even if you have a terrible one, you can just use that to set up the really phenomenal game that you have coming next, and the difference will make it seem all the more amazing to the players.

If you could give any tips or bits of advice to someone younger than you who wants to be a DM, what would you say?

JEN: Do it. Just go have fun. You know, use your imagination and play. Try to play like childhood make-believe, you know? Just get out there and enjoy it, and remember that these games are for everyone. There are games for everyone and there are ways to participate for everyone. So yeah, bring your imagination to it, and just have fun with it. Don't worry so much about whether you're doing it right.

You know the first page of the 5e *Player's Handbook* talks about how you don't need to know all the rules to play D&D. That it's about building the relationships and the story, like the relationships with your friends at the table and the story that you're building together. That's the core of what this game is, and I couldn't agree more. You know that's what it's about, so go in and build those stories and have those adventures because they'll stay with you forever.

But I think it's also really important to be able to let people know what you need in that sphere and also to respect what other people need because that often, to me, is the difference between a good game and a bad game. It is when you feel like you are being heard and respected at a table and supported—that makes all the difference.

Is there anything else that you really want to add?

JEN: Yeah, I think there's something I want to add for DMs and especially for people who want to make games or stream games or, you know, take things to a different level than just playing in a home game—but it applies to home games, too—and that is to find the stories that excite you and that only you can tell. There are so many people playing these games, which is so wonderful, but there's only one of you. It sounds so cheesy, but there's only one of you with the experiences that you've had and who thinks about things in the way you think and who imagines things in the way you imagine them, so tell those stories because no one else can. That's what makes the games and this space really special. Create the games that you think are really cool because it just speaks to something about how you see the world or how you would like to see the world.

CHAPTER FIVE

Session 0 and Safety Tools

WHEN WE SAY SESSION 0, we mean a couple of important things. First, it's the point in the setup of the game when you talk about expectations and limits. It's gathering your friends to talk about what you want and don't want, so you can all go on a great journey together. In D&D's fifth edition core rule book, there is a small section that gives you advice on how to do this. However, I am here to magnify and expand on these suggestions, guidelines, and hopefully the tools you want and need so that your table can tell the most incredible story possible.

Having a Session 0 before you start playing helps everyone manage their expectations. It's an opportunity to make a checklist of what your experience can and will be. That said, you can have a Session 0 at any time, not just before a campaign or when the game begins for the first time. You can have this session before any time you play to revisit rules, guidelines, the story, or the safety tools with your table.

Subjects, Themes, and Mood

During your Session 0, it's important to know what kind of game your table wants to play, along with content preferences and expectations. Having everyone on the same page by discussing what story subjects, themes (sometimes also known as the genre), and moods you want to include will ensure you start the game off in sync. Here are a few examples! These examples don't have to relate to the option next to it and are all separate or can be mixed and matched in any way.

STORY SUBJECTS
Saving the world from danger
Preparing for a big celebration
Delivering a package to someone who really needs it and soon!

THEMES
Fantasy
Science fiction
Mystery

MOODS
Happy and full of jokes
Spooky and intense
Action-packed adventure

As often happens in TTRPGs, you might find that your subjects, themes, and moods morph as your characters and story expand, so it is always good to check in now and then to ensure everyone is still on board! It is a good idea to plan your Session 0 far enough ahead of your first session so that you can build what the game's story will be like as a party.

INSIGHT CHECK!

TTRPG DM and crafter extraordinaire Vee talks about some of her favorite themes for a game. You can read more about Vee in her interview on page 82.

• • • •

VEE: Please give me fractured fairy tales and going into the deep, dark woods and playing around with different creatures and lore. I love that type of thing! I honestly like Baba Yaga as my go-to. Love using her. She's not necessarily my big baddie. But I definitely tap into old folklore from my background from doing English and literature and everything like that. So, I will sometimes even go back to old lore that people forget, like I'll use the original Grimm fairy tale books.

Safety Tools

Sometimes games have content or situations where a player or GM may feel stressed out, unsafe, or otherwise not having fun. Safety tools are a way for players and GMs to communicate and check-in before, during, and after a game in order to make sure everyone is still having fun, and to provide the right support when needed.

—THE TTRPG SAFETY TOOLKIT

Before starting a game, you should absolutely look into what safety tools you would like to use or that are made available with the game or games you play. Everyone at your table should feel as safe and comfortable as possible, so if you are having trouble finding the tools you want to use, you can also come up with your own. Remember that while you might think the story you are telling is fun, it could have something that someone at the table finds incredibly scary or gross or makes them feel uncomfortable, and sometimes those feelings can take away from the fun they might have been having.

Invite your guardian to your Session 0 to suggest ideas, and ask if they would be okay with helping you take notes about what the group wants. This way if there are any big questions or discussions, you have someone there to help!

You can discuss this game directly and share as much as feels important, but also don't forget to include some sort of safety tool(s) at your table. These will help you figure out what the game will be like before you start playing and help keep a good pace based on your wants, needs, and desires in this game even after the Session 0.

ROLL WITH ADVANTAGE!

Whether you're the storyteller or a member of the party, everyone should agree on what safety tools to use so they know what to do if they start to feel uncomfortable or need to stop playing the game for a moment. It is very important to remember that safety tools are not made to restrict your game; they are made so that you know how to expand your games in ways that everyone at your table enjoys. If one person says they're afraid of spiders, then it's your responsibility to make sure the game doesn't include spiders—even if no one else is afraid or everyone else thinks spiders are cool and wants to have them in the game.

Safety tools should be agreed upon during the Session 0; however, the themes, topics, or items the group agrees that they don't want in the game might change as you play, and new ones might come up too. For example, when exploring a deep, dark cave, the players are asked to crawl through a very tight tunnel to get to the next room. During this moment in the game, a player says something or uses the agreed-upon safety tool to show that they are not comfortable. With no questions asked, the narrator should stop the scene, make sure the player is okay, and maybe have everyone take a break. Then after the break, the game can continue with either a revised version of the scene or with a time skip, so that scene doesn't happen again.

Below are a few different types of safety tools that you and your table can use. You might decide to use only one or even mix and match tools, depending on what your table agrees on. You might decide to use tools that you and an older family member found online or even ones that you and your table make especially for yourselves! The most important thing is that everyone can have the best time possible in the safest way.

LINES AND VEILS

A really important tool is lines and veils, which are about what stuff you do or don't want to be in the games you're playing. You make a list and you share it with everyone at the table. If you're only comfortable sharing it with the storyteller or even a guardian who is around for the session, that's important.

Lines are things that you don't want to see in the game you play at all. For example, a line might be seeing someone get really sick because you have a bad memory with it or you have bad memories related to other people with it. You don't want to see that in your game, and you want to make sure that everyone else knows how you feel about it, so that they can respect that and not bring it up.

Veils are things that you don't want to focus on but you might be okay with in small amounts (or that take place "off camera," which is when a narrator says it happened but doesn't go into detail), and you just establish that with your party. Using the same example as before, maybe you don't mind knowing someone got sick, but you just don't want it to go any further than that.

So, a line is when a player or narrator, well, draws a line and says that they don't want certain things to appear in the game at all, and a veil is something that the player or narrator

MAKE A
BRAVERY ROLL

There are a bunch of common fears (or phobias) that people might not want to face in their game. When you sit down with a table to play a game, pull out a piece of paper and talk out with the table what things they want to keep. You can even start the list with a few common ones like spiders, ghosts, or blood. Bring those up to start the list, and then you know what everyone agrees they're okay with having in the game! For this activity, make a list of things you'd want to check in with your table to see what they might be nervous or afraid of so you can have it ready!

is okay with but only if they use small details or it happens off screen. Remember, unless you feel comfortable sharing, you don't have to explain why something is a line or a veil. Respecting everyone at the table also means considering their feelings and understanding that they might not want to talk about why they don't like or are afraid of things.

Lines and veils help everyone at the table know what stuff people don't want to see to avoid approaching it. It's good to have that conversation before you play, and it's good to keep having that conversation because some of that stuff might change. A new line might pop up after something happens in the game. A line might later become a veil, or the opposite. Checking in with that stuff occasionally is good because then everyone knows what the entire table is comfortable with.

THUMBS-UP

When you are having a good time and enjoying something that's happening, feel free to give the narrator and the table a thumbs-up. The narrator can also use this to quickly check in that everyone else at the table is having fun in the moment and is comfortable to see where it goes. You can also use the thumbs-down to signal to the table and the narrator if something happens that you don't enjoy or that makes you feel uncomfortable.

PICTURES AND VISUALS

This is a tool where you print out or draw faces with different emotions on them. This is something that Questlings does that I really enjoy. Then, at any point the narrator can ask how the party is doing, or a member of the party can show that they are uncomfortable by pointing at or holding one of the faces that represents how they're feeling—whether that is happy, sad, or frustrated.

INSIGHT CHECK!

Game designer Justice talks about the safety tools in his game Questlings! You can read more about Justice in his interview on page 108.

• • • •

JUSTICE: We made our tools more visual, and they relied heavily on making it so that the players had something to point at because sometimes it can be scary to say things out loud, especially if you're a kid and even if you're an older kid.

When I say not knowing the words for specific things, I mean sometimes you can feel a feeling and not know how to explain it. Adults have issues verbalizing their feelings all the time! Feelings are big and scary.

Not knowing how to say the thing can be really frustrating, so we have visuals for players, so they can point to how they're feeling. We had a sad face, an angry face, a meh face, and a smiley face, so if players are feeling like "I'm having a lot of fun" they can point to the green smiling face, or the meh face if they're not really interested, or the angry or sad face.

Having that visual and letting players know they're allowed to point to these at any time and that it's okay was super important. We had that right on the character sheet and wanted it to be accessible and easy for anyone who wanted those, so they were always there. Having these tools makes people more creative. When you're storytelling and you have these parameters and things to think about, it motivates you to be more creative and work around that.

X, O, N CARDS

These are another way to check in. The O card is for when you're having a good time. It is a good way to show that yes everything is okay and you enjoy the scene, you enjoy the roleplaying that people are doing, and nothing is making you uncomfortable or sad in it.

The N card signifies a bit more of a neutral feeling. You're not necessarily loving what's happening in the scene, or you don't mind where it is now but you don't want it to go any further. Someone might have said something that didn't make you upset, but it's not the story that you're having fun with.

The X card is for when something happened or is happening and you want a hard stop in this moment or the scene or the story. If someone uses an X card, then it is a good idea to take a break and make sure that the person doesn't need or want to talk to the group or an older family member before continuing.

STARS AND WISHES

This tool comes from a writer named Lu Quade, and it's meant to help everyone at the table share their feelings about how the session or game went. He describes the process of stars and wishes like this: "At the conclusion of a game session, everyone who played offers a Star to another player, to a moment in the game, or to an element of the overall experience (you can give out more stars if you have time). You can award a star for amazing roleplay, great character moments, amazing descriptions by the GM, the feeling you had at a certain moment, another player's generosity, a mechanic of the game system that really sang, et cetera." A star is a thing you loved about the game, and if the game you played was amazing, it is often hard to choose!

After stars have been given, everyone makes a wish. Each player tells the table something they would like to see happen in a future session. You can make a wish about something you want to see happen with your own character, an interaction you'd love to see between two characters, a mechanic you would like to see come into play that you haven't seen yet, places you hope the story might go, and so on.

Using stars and wishes is a great way to tell others what stuff made the session fun for you, and it helps the entire table know what you want to see more of in the game in a positive way.

As I stated earlier in the chapter, these are only a few of the different tools that are available, but they can make a big difference in your experience, and I hope you use them at your table.

CHAPTER SIX

Tools of the Trade

NOW THAT YOU'VE PICKED OUT your game, you have a party, and you have the tools to play safely, you want to see what other ways you can explore the world of tabletop roleplaying games. One of the great things about tabletop RPGs is that there are so many ways to bring extra fun to your table. Whether it is a set of special dice or a hand-painted miniature or just a cool hat and a great accent, you can use the following "tools." Of course, none of them are necessary, but some games might benefit from, or you might find it useful to have . . .

IMAGINATION

- This is seriously one of the most important parts of all TTRPGs. You might not have maps or miniatures, and you might need a digital dice roller because you don't have any dice, but you can always imagine the world. The storyteller may just tell you "The person is in the other room" but doesn't have an actual map to show you, so your imagination really comes into use here. In TTRPGs, using your imagination in this way is also called "Theatre of the Mind," which refers to the power you have to create an image in your head that captures what's happening without having pieces to move around or images to see.

- Remember, those physical pieces can make a game unique and interesting or help to process it, but using your imagination to visualize it yourself is one of the most useful tools you can have. Luckily, it is one that will always be with you.

PEN AND PAPER

- Having a pen (or pencil) and a piece of paper will be very handy when playing a tabletop roleplaying game. This will be useful for any notes that you might want to take about the story as well as writing down anything you'll need for your character, so that you can remember all your information! You can also use these tools to sketch out maps as the narrator explains them, remember details about monsters or NPCs, and even draw your own character to share with the table.

MAPS

- Any time you want to move characters around an area or represent where a scene is taking place, you can use a map! These are also called battle mats, or grid maps if they have a grid. There are detailed maps that can be found at your local game store, but you can be creative and make your own!

- Take a blank piece of paper and draw out the scenery however you like. If you ask a guardian, they can also help you find images to print out and add to your map to help add in the details you might want for your session.

DICE SETS

- If you ever want to buy dice, you'll often find them in sets! General dice sets come with a D4, D6, D8, D10, D12, and D20 and can be found at comic book and game stores as well as online. You'll also find dice sets that include a handful of D10s, or you might even find bags of dice with a random assortment and plenty of different colors—those are the most fun to get because they are always a surprise.

- Dice sets also come in many different materials including plastic, metal, and even stone! Some dice makers will create custom dice for you or to match your character—a set of green dice with flowers inside sounds like the perfect fit for a druid or a set of black smokey dice with red numbers for a rogue.

MINIATURES

- Generally, these are small, molded plastic figures used to represent characters or objects in a game. There are game stores and websites where, with the help of an older family member, you can find and buy different miniatures, which are also called "minis," of different sizes, shapes, and character types. They can be two dimensional or three dimensional; some come with paint and some without!

- Certain games will even have specific minis made for them. People will add terrain pieces to make maps interesting. Have you ever seen those tiny sets families put out around the holidays with cars or trees or rocks? Those sorts of things are designed for tabletop roleplaying playing too! There are bundles, castles, and carriages.

No matter what assortment of tools you take from this chapter to use in your own games, they will make games even better and more fun. They don't come in any direct order, and no list is required for you to have fun your way. The thing about tools is there are different tools for different jobs, and once you figure out what job you're working on, it should be easier to pick and choose the tools you need for it. There are a lot more optional tools you can add to your toolbox too that aren't physical objects you use in the game or on a game board. They can be things you bring or do!

Dressing Up as Your Character

It is extremely common for people playing a tabletop game together to fully dress up or wear a few special items to help them embody their character. It might be a wig or maybe even a full outfit or costume, or it might just be some makeup, or (with the glory of the internet) it could even just be filters for a webcam. It helps some people feel more in character, and other people it just gives more confidence.

INSIGHT CHECK!

GABE: I've often dressed up as my characters because I definitely feel more confident if I am wearing a fancy suit like my character when playing a detective game (for example), and I can almost use my outfit as a prop. I can tip my hat, or adjust my jacket, and it still feels in character, plus it gives me a little courage.

If you aren't a fan of the idea of dressing up in person, you can create a digital character, or avatar, to share. There are websites that can help you build your digital character for when you play online. Some tabletop roleplaying gamers also use them when streaming or in videos so that the audience can see the character instead of the player. One option is Hero Forge, where you can create a digital miniature of your character and save a picture! Another is One More Multiverse, where you can make a digital version of your character with 2D (two-dimensional) art! While it might not seem the same as dressing up, having a digital character is still a way for a player to depict or present their characters to others, so, in a way, it's like digital cosplay. Remember to check in with your guardian before creating and sharing your digital character online.

When you're figuring out how to depict your character, remember that there's no right or wrong way to do it. Some people do it just for fun or because it helps them get into character. If your character wears an eye patch but wearing an eye patch makes you feel uncomfortable, then you don't have to wear it. If your character has six arms, you don't need six arms . . . unless you want them!

If you find a group that loves to just dress up whenever they meet to play a game just because it's fun, then that's amazing. And if you're with a group that doesn't want to do that, don't worry because that is okay too. You might even be in a group that is mixed, with some players who like to dress up and some who don't. Before you dress up in your group, ask the table if anyone would mind if you dress up a little the next time you play. If that's something you're interested in, ask your table and see if others might want to do it too. You might be surprised to find out that a few other people might want to dress up with you! Making sure that everyone is comfortable and having fun is what matters at the end of the day.

So, do you think you would cosplay as a character that you want to play?

ROLL WITH ADVANTAGE!

Check out *A Kid's Guide to Fandom: Exploring Fan-Fic, Cosplay, Gaming, Podcasting, and More in the Geek World!* by Amy Ratcliffe and read the chapter about cosplay for more information and inspiration!

Voices and Artwork

When you have an idea of what your character looks like, if you don't use an online tool to make art, then you can draw them! Grab a piece of paper, something to draw with (maybe colored pencils), and start sketching out what they might look like! Include their outfit and anything they might be carrying. You can create different outfits they might wear on different days, even pajamas. You can draw different hairstyles or different faces they make if they're happy or sad. It doesn't have to be perfect, and you don't have to show anyone else if you don't want to. The more you practice, the better you'll get at it, and the easier it'll be to start showing what your character looks like through artwork.

So, you know what your character looks like, and whether they fight and what they fight with, and what their hobbies are. Dressing up is one way to bring your character to life, and another is to give them their own voice. As with everything else in this chapter, just remember that it doesn't have to be perfect, fancy, or really wild, but even doing something small to distinguish your character's voice can be really fun.

INSIGHT CHECK!

GABE: One of the hardest things for me is doing a voice. That said, I like doing it, and sometimes I realize that just making my voice deeper is just enough to get the character to where I want them to be. Remember, a character's voice can just be your voice, that is always okay!

When you are working on character creation, think about what they sound like. Maybe they are businesslike, so they have a more serious voice. When you're trying to figure out the character's voice, think about whether something has affected their voice. For example, maybe this character has a gigantic dragon inside of them and that dragon has a deep voice that comes out sometimes. Or maybe your character doesn't really speak at all because they are more reserved, so their voice might be soft and whispery. If you are playing a younger character, then maybe they have a higher-pitched, more excited voice.

Of course, you are always discovering and figuring out your character every time you play them. However, if trying to come up with or using a voice becomes too much work or not fun, then it is okay to take a break for a while. You can describe to the table what tone your character is speaking in without having to stress out: "They're saying this in a very angry way." "They're really excited when they say this." Those extra notes can help clarify!

Painting Miniatures

The world of miniatures is vast! There are miniatures that are figurines, terrains, and props, and even miniatures that are effects of stuff happening in the world like fire or wind or even a tidal wave! Also, just because they are called miniatures doesn't mean that they are tiny! In fact, the average miniature is twenty-five or twenty-eight centimeters tall.

Figure miniatures are called tokens when they represent a character from the party or an NPC. Sometimes a narrator might set out tokens to represent the different characters, which is helpful for counting how many people are there (both friend and foe), to get a better idea of what's happening, and to see the scene in real life. Of course, miniatures aren't necessary, but they are a great tool to help the table visualize what is going on in the game. If you are interested in miniatures, don't feel like you have to get the ones that are made specifically for tabletop games because they are often expensive, despite how cool they are. Instead, get creative!

You can use basically anything for your miniatures, for example, things that you already might have in your room: little LEGO Minifigures could represent your party and NPCs, and maybe a toy monster can stand in for your big bad. Even the little packs of toy animals at the craft store can be helpful. Outside of tabletop gaming, people will build miniatures of towns and zoos, or shops, or even ice skating rinks, especially around the holidays, and they might have a store on Etsy where they sell figurines or objects you can use for your game. You can also just make your own miniatures out of clay or paper if you feel like it! Anything you have can be a miniature to represent something for your games. I've used a mug to represent a huge well and a red scarf to represent an entire forest on fire. Get creative!

If you do want to buy a miniature, then head to your nearest hobby or board game store, but remember that they come in all different sizes, shapes, and materials—including metal! You will find two main types of miniatures in the store: painted and unpainted.

The painted ones will usually cost a little bit more just because they already come, well, painted. Someone has already put color on them and done little bits of detail to make it look cool and come to life. That said, it can be a lot of fun painting your own miniature! There is even a whole community that loves painting miniatures so much they actually spend more time painting than playing the tabletop roleplaying games the miniatures are for. If you decide to paint your own miniature, then make sure you talk to the store staff. They can probably give you a few tips or advice about the best paint and brushes to use.

Even if you have miniatures that you haven't painted because you're not ready, that's still totally fine. You can paint them at your own pace. Remember, though, that if you make a mistake or decide you want to do something different, you can always paint over it and try again! The nice thing about painting a miniature is that after it dries you can make changes or start over if you'd really like to. Be bold and paint it your way!

ROLL WITH ADVANTAGE!

—— INTERVIEW ——

VEE THE CRAFTING MUSE
(SHE/HER)

Introduce yourself.

> **VEE:** I am Vee the muse. I am a professional DM and player as well as partner manager at Codename Entertainment known for Idle Champions, and I have been a longtime artist and mini painter as well.

Do you remember how you started playing tabletop roleplaying games?

> **VEE:** It was completely by accident. I've always been a fan of reading because I have an English literature background and major. So, I have been reading fantasy novels since I was small and had started playing a couple video games like *Baldur's Gate* and *Champions of Norrath*, and then I got pulled into playing the tabletop stuff later on in life. Then, I found D&D in college, and that's when I started getting more into learning about it and finding out about it.

How did you get started painting minis?

> **VEE:** I actually got started painting minis when I was a little kid, but they were more like porcelain miniatures and little character miniatures. Things like *My Little Pony* and things that I would sculpt out of various clays and papier-mâché and make my own little miniature creatures. So that's actually something I've been doing since I was young and then when I found out that with tabletop games miniatures are

involved, I was like, "Oh, I could do this. Let me do this." And I jumped right in and I painted a gargoyle from Hero's Quest and it hooked me.

Do you have any tips for newcomers?

VEE: Don't get scared by having it be perfect from the word go. Mini painting, like any learned skill, takes time. Yes, you can have some artistry to it later on down the line, but whenever you're learning something new, remember that you have to start somewhere. So, I always recommend you start with a larger miniature and don't go for the itty-bitty ones. You know, like a halfling artificer type of thing. Don't do that because you'll make yourself bonkers. It's better to start with a larger creature to make it easier to learn how to work with paints on the mini and have a little bit more space to work with.

It also helps just to get your basic colors: black, white, brown, red, blue, and yellow because, guess what, you can take red, blue, and yellow and mix your colors together. It is also a good way to learn your color wheels and information like that. Then you have your black and white and brown to play around with and learn how to get tones. So, you can actually get started for a very small amount of money. You can just get the cheap craft brushes from department stores or grocery stores and start there.

Then once you get a feel for it, you'll be able to tell if this is something you want to keep doing or if maybe you want to try a different approach. You can also learn a lot from watching a bunch of different mini painters on YouTube because you may find someone paints more in the way you want to stylistically than someone else might.

You mentioned being a DM and player—is it scary being a DM to you?

VEE: I thought it was going to be, which is why I was very reluctant to be one in the beginning. Once I started to DM, I actually realized this is storytelling with friends, and you kind of get to guide the story. So, once I realized that, it was amazing and it was so much fun. Sometimes you're going to have to stop and go back and look at a rule if you want to, or you can check it out later after the fact, but the most important part is that everyone's having fun and that you're getting people excited about a journey and an adventure.

What was a moment when you realized you wanted to do more tabletop?

VEE: Oh wow, that's a good question. It was probably the first stream I was actually on. I was playing with a bunch of other crafters, and I realized people were talking about my character after the fact, and I was like, "Wait . . . you like her, too?" So, it was a whole experience sharing a character and seeing people's reactions and hearing what they're connecting with from that character. That's really cool because I connected with that too because obviously I created the character myself, and that's when I realized this is something more than just something you do for yourself, you get to share it with others.

What's some advice you want to pass on to someone who is new to minis?

VEE: Find the joy in the play and don't get caught up in doing it right. There are so many different types of paint, different colors, and different brands that they come in. Find the one that's right for you. Find the one that's easy to work with and the one that's fun with the colors you like the most. Also find the brushes that work for you, and if it doesn't come out perfect the first time, be creative and have fun. If the arm is different color than you meant it to be, maybe there's a reason in the story why that happened. This friendly elf has a red arm because they fell into a magic bag of berries and now their arm is strawberry scented!

Maps and Terrain

Depending on who you're talking to, the terrain means the playing field, map, or the individual squares you put miniatures on, or it could be specifically about physical pieces that you might place on the map, like buildings or trees. What makes using the terrain so fun is that it helps you imagine how your character might interact and move about in the game world.

If you are the narrator of the table, you have a lot to consider when it comes to the terrain. In fact, there's an infinite number of possibilities based on your imagination. For example, your party may start inside a castle but then head to a deep and dark dungeon. Then, after the dungeon, they may end up exploring a tropical forest. Being able to show the different terrain of those areas can be really nice for the players. That said, your terrain doesn't have to be over the top. Maybe draw a map of parts of the castle or the one room that the party might be in the most. Or maybe you have a few plastic toy trees you can set down at the table to give them the sense they are in a forest.

There is nothing wrong with using homemade pieces, repurposing toys or other items from your room, or just getting creative! You can use a stick you found outside, and now it is an amazing fallen tree. A couple of small pebbles are now some really cool boulders. Don't be afraid to get creative and have fun building up this world!

GRIDS

A lot of tabletop games, especially roleplaying games, are played using grid maps. Grid maps very often go hand in hand with miniature terrains and miniatures because they help give players an idea of space and distance. For some tabletop roleplaying games, knowing how many spaces a player or NPC can move, how far an attack or magic can go, or the size of a room or an outdoor space is really important. Of course, your map doesn't have to have a grid if you don't want! Using your imagination is just as much fun.

There are a few different types of grids you can use if you and the table want to, like a regular square grid, a hex or isometric grid, or even a map that has no grid! A regular grid looks a lot like a chessboard (and honestly it sometimes kind of feels like one too), while a hex or isometric grid looks more like a honeycomb. "Hex" is short for "hexagon," which is a shape with six sides and six angles.

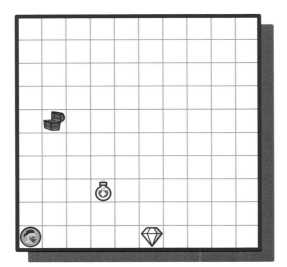 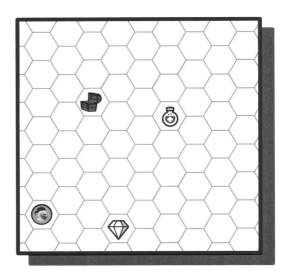

On hex grids you can move more than just up and down, left and right, because now you have four possible sides to move. Now you have diagonal up and diagonal down on either side. This is nice because it gives everyone at your table more options when it comes to movements and directions, but it can sometimes feel a little more complicated too.

MAP IT OUT

Yes, yes, I know this does kind of feel like math. However, this is one of those weird moments where math is really useful. In this activity, you are going to learn how to measure distance on a grid map to find some treasure!

On the previous grid maps, there are three spaces with different treasures: a diamond, a healing potion, and a handful of gold coins. Now, before we start, we are going to say that one space represents ten feet. The square grid map is ten squares by ten squares, which means that from one side to the other represents one hundred feet across. Take a miniature or a token to represent you, and place it on the bottom-left corner of the square grid. Your goal is to figure out how many feet away each of the treasures is from you!

Before you get started, here are a few things to remember:

- Each grid space equals ten feet.
- You don't count the space where your miniature is standing, but you do count the space where it will be standing at the end of your turn.
- You can only move up, down, left, or right. This means you can only move in a straight line, not diagonally.

Okay, now go!

If you got all the distances right, then congratulations, and if you got them wrong, don't worry! Just take another look at the square grid map and see if you can figure out what you might have missed. Believe me, many players get counting wrong, more often than you think. It is really tricky sometimes!

When you solve the square grid, try to gather the treasures from the hex grid. The same rules apply as above, only this time, you can move up, down, left, right, and diagonally! Take your time, and good luck!

These exercises are great for explaining and learning how to move and measure distance on a grid map. So, if you are looking for more grid fun, you can make your own grid map problem for your table to solve. All you need is some grid paper, a pencil, and your imagination. See, math can be a lot of fun when you're playing games!

Square Grid Answer Key

Diamond: 5 square spaces (50 ft.)

Health potion: 5 square spaces (50 ft.)

Gold coin: 6 square spaces (60 ft.)

Hex Grid Answer Key

Diamond: 3 hex spaces (30 ft.)

Health potion: 6 hex spaces (60 ft.)

Gold coin: 5 hex spaces (50 ft.)

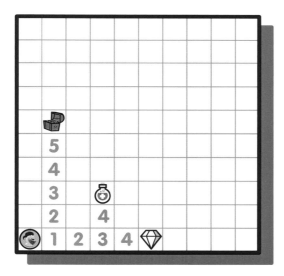
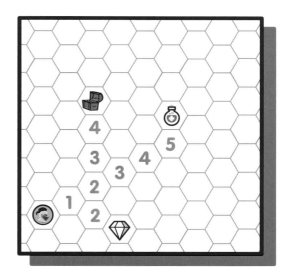

CHAPTER SEVEN

Making Your Own Games

MAKING A GAME MEANS CREATING a world people can play in, and we've talked about the incredible diversity that exists in games over these previous chapters. Don't forget that you have the creativity to do it, so let's talk about what goes into doing it. In order to have tabletop roleplaying game, someone has to be out there making them. That's where game designers come in. Sometimes a tabletop game will have a handful of people making it, and other times it involves a team of nearly a dozen different creators. Game artists, writers, testers, and editors—these are just some of the general roles that make up a team behind a tabletop game.

When you're making a game, you don't have to have everything figured out from the get-go. You might only have an idea in your head that you want to roll a specific type of die and then something happens. That's more than okay, that's a start! If you created a small list that made things happen depending on what number a player rolls on a D6, that's a game! You can add to the plot, you can switch up the dice, or you can change the chart they roll on depending on different situations. Try making something small at first, because you can always add to it or change something later on. Try out dice or cards or even saying words out loud. Try out a few options, and when you find one that you really like, lean into it!

INSIGHT CHECK!

GABE: I love having the ability to come up with worlds and ideas and shape them into something fun or interesting. There is nothing more fun than being able to create the story behind why the continent exists and explain what the animals are like on it. Or to have the chance to define why a specific group of travelers wanders where they do and what knowledge they have, or the opportunity to describe an underground cavern where eight-legged wolves search the darkness for secret gems. Getting a chance to tell these kinds of stories is so much fun to me, but it isn't always easy. It takes a lot of practice and making a few mistakes along the way. Practice and practice and find something that you're really excited about because the greatest stories come from ideas that are important to you in some way.

An important word to remember when thinking about your game before you get started is "scope." This means how big your idea is going to be. Figuring out the scope of the game will help outline how much work you'll need to do and what kinds of ideas or mechanics or themes you need to focus on as you create. For example, if you want to build a character's home, there is a big difference between thinking about a small town and a major city.

For a small town, it might be more important to have all the details of the NPCs and backstory of the town worked out, while for a major city you might not have to. However, with a larger city there are also more opportunities to have characters meet new people, try new things, and so on, than maybe they could in a smaller town. The same idea of scope goes for thinking about your game's story—do you want a longer story that is told over many sessions, or is this a shorter story that can be told in only a few hours?

There are a variety of types and sizes of games that you can make—your imagination is the limit! In fact, a great way to get started with making your own game is a homebrew or a micro-game.

Homebrews

A homebrew is extra, unofficial content that people in the TTRPG community make to add something special to their favorite game. Many people make homebrews to add things they think are missing from their game, whether that is a new class, job, adventure, item, or anything else they can think of. Telling your own unique story with rules from an officially published game can be considered a homebrew! In fact, people love to design extra things for Dungeons & Dragons. Although the official content is designed by Wizards of the Coast, there is so much more designed by other people to help make the game more fun. The traditional rules might tell you how you should play your wizard, but if you want to change it and play it a different way, that doesn't make it wrong! You're just making it more fun and accessible for you to play.

HOMEBREWS TO TRY

Witch+Craft, by Astrolago Press ✳ Witchcraft: Magic of Hereva, by Xacur ✳ The Wild Sheep Chase, by Winghorn Press ✳ The Hidden Halls of Hazakor, by Insane Angel Studios

Now that you know what a homebrew is, let's create your own dragon to add to your next D&D game. There are so many different dragons to take inspiration from, so don't forget to think about ones you've seen or learned about in cartoons, books, video games, and movies as you work on your unique homebrew dragon!

CREATE A DRAGON!

To create a dragon, all you have to do is answer a few questions:

- How big is your dragon? _____ _____

- Where does it live? _____ _____

- What is your dragon's favorite food? _____ _____

- What does it look like? _____ _____

- What color or colors does your dragon have? _____ _____

- Does it have any magic powers? (Can it turn invisible, change size, etc.?) _____

  _____

- Is it nice or mean? _____

  _____

- Does it breathe out anything special? (Fire, ice, or maybe candy?) _____

  _____

- What is your dragon's name? _____

  _____

Draw a picture of your dragon below!

Micro-Games

Okay, but what if you want to create your own original game? Well, a good place to start would be with a micro-game! Also known as one-shot TTRPGs, these are games that can be played in a single session, or in less than three hours. Sometimes a table will interrupt their main story with a one-shot game and treat it almost like a cool side quest or adventure! When you start thinking of your own ideas, they don't have to be super big or really long. They can be something you start and finish in just one hangout with friends! Something nice about one-shots is, if not everyone can hang out next time, then at least you finished this little story now.

When you're designing your game and figuring out how long you want it to be, a good strategy can be to design a one-shot, and if it feels like there's a lot more story to tell or adventure to have, then you can expand on it from there.

MICRO- OR ONE-SHOT GAMES TO TRY

Honey Heist, by Grant Howitt ✳ Lasers & Feelings, by John Harper ✳
Maze Rats, by Questing Beast Games ✳ *The Ultimate*
Micro-RPG Book, by James D'Amato

INSIGHT CHECK!

How did you get started creating and playing tabletop roleplaying games?

GABE: I used to think being interested in tabletop roleplaying games was a bad thing. I used to be really shy about it, so when I was in school, I would start writing down ideas and stories and stuff. I wrote stories about people fighting dragons; I wrote stories about people flying around through space, stories about spies. I wrote a whole bunch of stories, and I wanted to enjoy them, but I didn't know ways that I could do it without just people reading it. So I would make things like the Choose Your Own Adventure book series, where you write the story, and then people can select an option a or an option b or an option c, and they go to that page for that option. Little did I realize those experiences are a lot like making a board game or tabletop RPG!

Then, when I was older, I discovered that tabletop roleplaying games existed and that they sometimes were my favorite parts of board games, and so just as I was leaving high school I wrote a really complicated, really fancy science fiction space game. It was not good, but it was a learning experience. I don't really talk about it much, but I even got it printed into a tiny physical notebook. I keep it as a reminder that I can be proud of the first thing I wrote, even if it's not my favorite. I started somewhere and I'm just getting better.

After that, I kept writing down my ideas and talking about them online or getting friends to play it and see what stuff they did or didn't like, and it helped me become a better designer, and I feel like after a while people started seeing something they liked and were impressed with and more people gathered to support me and my ideas, which helped me get to where I am now!

Being Respectful

Creating homebrews and micro-games is a lot of fun, and there are entire companies whose whole job is to create new homebrew content for D&D 5e. However, just because you can create new content for your favorite game doesn't mean that there aren't rules and guidelines that you should follow. The rules might be different depending on the game that you are adding new stuff for, and depending on whether you are just making something for fun or you want to share and sell it. It is always a good idea to talk to a guardian about your ideas and make sure that you are following the correct guidelines so that you respect the hard work of the original creators! This is just like plagiarism in school. You can't just copy someone else's work.

If you are thinking about creating a homebrew or a micro-game using the mechanics or other elements from another game, then you can't just automatically use any rules that they already have out in the books. The rules already exist in those books but you can come up with new rules if it gives you permission to do so and you acknowledge where it came from. This is important to respect the creator of the work but also because when making something original, it becomes unique coming from your mind. Instead, you should look at the list of rules called the system reference document, or the SRD. This is a collection of rules and mechanics from the game that you are allowed to reference when creating something new. You can think of it as rules to follow so that your new content fits within the world and mechanics of the original game.

That said, you can also use the SRDs from different games to help you come up with something new and interesting. If you share your work, though, it is always a good idea to make sure you give credit to the original games! Knowing what you can and can't work with from a game you love can change how you think about your game and its scope, but that is just part of the process!

INSIGHT CHECK!

What advice do you have for people who want to make games?

GABE: Use the world around you for inspiration. Use the stories that you like that made you laugh or made you smile or even made you cry that you remember because they were a good story. Learn to use the world around you, but make sure you're not just copying it. Don't just take someone else's idea; learn from their ideas, and if someone else's idea inspires you, that's a great way to spark your creativity.

If you heard about my first character and that inspired you to want to make a character like him, then make a character like him! How is your character different than mine? Maybe they're also a person with magic that came from a dragon, but change the dragon. Is it from the sky, from the earth, from water? How big is your dragon? Is your character not an elf but maybe a lizard person or a tiny goblin? Take the inspiration and create something unique and wonderful from it.

Plenty of people will probably have done something similar to what you might be thinking of, but what makes something interesting is the unique way you approach it. Your individual perspective is what's going to make it stick out. Plus, make things that you're excited about. There's a big difference when you make something that you really care about and something that is not important to you. Give people the chance to be excited with you, and those are the people you probably want to play your games. At least that's been my experience.

Making Your Own Game

You've been reading about ways people have made their own games and hopefully have started to think about games you like playing and what mechanics are in them, so let's come up with an idea for your own game! Remember, there's no "right" way to make a game. In fact, designers have many different ways of doing things, and they might work differently based on what works best for their team or the type of game that they are trying to make. The best thing to do to get your creative energy flowing is to think about what makes you happy when you play a game or what kinds of things you like about your favorite games.

WHAT GAME
WOULD YOU MAKE?

Getting started making a game can be tough, but that is where this cool quiz comes in. Circle the answer that best fits what you want to do, or if you are feeling adventurous, roll a die or pick randomly, and see what kind of game you get!

What kind of theme/genre do you want?

  1. Fantasy

  2. Science fiction

  3. Everyday

  4. Historical

  5. Mystery

  6. Haunted

What is the tone of your game?

1. Happy

2. Spooky

3. Funny

4. Cute

5. Scary

6. Romantic

What tools do you want to have in your game?

1. Dice

2. Playing cards

3. Saying words out loud

4. Miniatures

5. Journal or notebook

6. Tarot or oracle cards

What do you want players to do in your game?

1. Solve puzzles

2. Fight creatures and villains

3. Tell stories

4. Explore someplace new

5. Work together

6. Compete

Do you want to have a narrator?

1. Narrator

2. No narrator

3. Take turns narrating

How long do you want your game to be?

1. Micro (less than three hours)

2. One-shot (one session)

3. Medium (two or three sessions)

4. Long (four or five sessions)

5. Campaign (more than five sessions/ongoing)

How big do you want the table to be?

1. 1 person / solo

2. 2 people

3. 3–4 people

4. 5–6 people

5. 7+ people

Now take your answers from the activity and start writing down any interesting ideas or characters you might have for your new game! Take ten, fifteen, or even thirty minutes and write down as many ideas as you can. If you start to run out of ideas or you get stuck, here are some questions you can ask yourself:

- What do you think is a good name for your game?
- What makes your game fun?
- What is something special about your game?
- Where does your game take place?
- Does your game have a story? What is it?
- How does your game start?
- How will players know when the game is over?
- Will the players need anything special to play your game?
- What tasks will the narrator have?
- Are there any interesting or special rules to your game?
- What does your game's art style look like?
- How many rules are there in your game? What are they?
- Do you have any safety tools you want to build into your game?
- How long do you expect a session to run?
- Do you want it to be a one-shot, have multiple sessions, or can it be either one?
- Will your players be learning anything new?
- What do you want people to experience in your game?
- What do you want your game to make players feel?

Take your time and write down as much as you want! Talk to your friends or an older family member about your game and see what they think—remember, it takes a lot of people to make a game. Once you've written everything down, take a break and come back to your answers after a day or two. Did you think of a new idea or change your mind about something? If so, that is completely normal and all part of the creative process. You want to make something that's good, not just fast. Also, don't forget that you can change things even after you might have thought it was done! That's okay! It's how different editions of games come to exist in the first place. Rarely do games stay in just one edition. Look at Dungeons & Dragons, for example. It is currently in its fifth edition, and its designers made so many changes to the rules and story because they're trying to improve the game experience even many years later. If they can make improvements, you absolutely are allowed to as well.

Once you feel like you've thought about your game enough, it is time to roll up your sleeves and get to work. Create or gather the different tools or pieces that your game needs (like cards, miniatures, or maps), and start working on the instructions and rule book. Don't forget to add some cool art and designs! This is a great time to ask your friends or table members if they want to help out as well, so that you can make something cool together.

Then it is time to do a playtest. This is when a game designer has a group of people play their new game to see how well it works. Maybe they thought having everyone take turns being the narrator was a great idea, but during the playtest the players find it too confusing.

This means the designer might go down to one narrator or tweak the game's rules to make it clearer how the players should trade off being the narrator. Playtests can be really fun but also really tough—especially if your game doesn't work exactly like you thought it would. Just remember that this is a chance for you to learn and make changes to improve your game. Most games go through multiple rounds of playtesting before they are finished, so don't get discouraged!

If you take all these bits and pieces and at least consider them, then you can definitely make a game of your own. Something else important, though, is to be proud of it. Even if it doesn't feel perfect or it isn't the most famous game, you made it! You took the time to write it and create it, and that's special! If you keep learning from playtesting and planning and writing, your game will get even better.

If you run out of ideas for it and can't add to it right now, that's alright! You can put it down, go play something else, go write something else, and come back to it. Your game and idea will be right there, and if you've written stuff down, then whenever you feel ready you can pick it back up. It should be as fun for you to make a game as it is for the people who play it. Remember that!

—— INTERVIEW ——

JUSTICE ARMAN
(HE/HIM)

Introduce yourself.

JUSTICE: My name is Justice Ramin Arman. I am a game designer in central Texas. I primarily work with D&D as a producer and as a game designer at Beadle and Grimm, where we make awesome box sets and other great products.

Do you remember how you started playing tabletop roleplaying games?

JUSTICE: It was 2013 and I was in college, and this guy who lived in my apartment complex knew I was kind of nerdy, and he asked me, "Hey, do you want to play in our Dungeons & Dragons game this Sunday? We need another player, and Brian thought you'd be a good person." And I was like, "Hmm, isn't it that the nerdy basement game where you have to dress up as knights?" He said, "Pretty much, but you can be anything you want to be," so I threw out this random off-the-cuff thing and asked if I could be a Minotaur named Beethoven who has a powdered wig and a harpsichord. It was just this ridiculous concept that I made up on the fly, and then he said, "Yeah, come over like an hour early and we'll get that made up and we'll play."

So, I played Beethoven for like a year, and I continued playing until I moved to game mastering, a year or two later.

Tell us more about Beethoven the Minotaur.

JUSTICE: Beethoven was a meme, a total meme, but I loved him. He had a musket, which the rules didn't support, but I think that was what was so fun about like playing tabletop.

So, my GM at the time was like, it takes a minute in real life to reload a musket, so if you have a musket, we'll let you reload in one round. So, every time we were in a fight I would just sit there patiently and say, "I'll reload this round." It wasn't until three months later somebody said, "You know, you don't have to have a musket. You'd be much better with a bow." I was like yeah, I don't know, I like the musket, that's what he's always used so why would I pick up a bow now?

He was cool. He had a powdered wig and was very buff. He was a former military captain or something, a Minotaur (a giant bull person), and he liked inventing things. So, every time that we would sit down and do downtime in a game, I would work on an invention. I was trying to make a grappling hook that blew up or something, and, by the end of that arc in our campaign, there was this door across a moat that we couldn't reach. Then I looked down and I had just finished this grappling hook like three sessions ago, and I was like, "It's time." This was what I'd been working toward, and I got that door down!

What was your first time DMing like?

JUSTICE: It was awesome and awkward, and I didn't like all of it at first. I had so much respect for my GM, who was one of my players at the table my first time. Things had gotten so busy for me at the time, but I wanted to just try to learn how to DM. I had the *Player's Handbook* and started by making my own world because that's what my GM did, and I had all these documents together and this big, loosely Western story planned out.

I remember making mistakes and being like, wow, this is actually really hard. My GM has been doing this all this time on the other side of that screen, and he knows these things so off the cuff. But he'd been playing D&D since he was eight years old and I'd been playing for a year at that time, maybe, but I remember it was fun. Everybody was chill and they laughed. They came over, and there were snacks, and it was in our apartment, and they played for multiple sessions. You know, looking back I don't think I've touched that world in I don't really know how long, but it was really nice of them to all like what I brought to the table. I look back on it now, and it was probably not the best game they probably had been in, but they were all chill. They all had a good time and so did I.

Do you feel like a more confident narrator after doing this for so long?

JUSTICE: I'm definitely a lot more comfortable now. A lot of—not all of it but a lot of—that creative energy that I used to put toward pure homebrew is now devoted to writing and getting paid for writing, and so I'd rather work on a framework that's already done, like a premade adventure, and spice it up. I remember early on I was running Storm King's Thunder, and after our sessions, I'd ask them, "Hey did you have fun? What did you like about the session?" And they tell me most of the time the stuff that excited them about this session, and usually it was the stuff that I had added to it. Which made me feel really happy. The energy that I put into it at the time, that I put into making something for their characters or making something I thought felt epic or setting them up for having those wins was the part that really resonated with them. I still have this guy who used to play in our group who I talked to every once in a while, and he always mentions our adventures. It was so fun, I wish we could all get back together and play again.

When the stuff that they liked was the stuff that I added I started feeling like maybe I'm not so terrible at this, but I still make mistakes now. I mean, that's life.

How did you get started creating **TTRPGs**?

JUSTICE: So, like 2015-ish I remember sitting in a Starbucks and I had opened LinkedIn. I was looking at the resumes of people who work at Wizards of the Coast and trying to make a connection, but I didn't know how to break into the industry. I was in a gap year in between deciding I didn't want to do medicine and I guess I got to use my public health degree, and I ended up working at that Starbucks.

While thinking about potentially trying to make that leap, that was when I moved to Beadle and Grimm full time, and that was like the end of my five-year plan at the time. I had saved up x amount of dollars, but opportunity comes knocking, and you have to take it because these jobs are like unicorns. You create and you work and you tell stories and write but you have to keep doing it even when it's hard or scary. I knew I loved doing stuff like this, but I had to keep looking for the opportunities and going for them when I could. I had to write on my own and also try to show why I would be a great member of a team to work with them too, and I started doing more and more projects by just going for those opportunities and showing what I could do. I mean the industry's getting bigger so hopefully these stories of people joining the industry will become more common.

Roll for Initiative

(Your Adventure Is Waiting)

THERE IS A WHOLE VARIETY of worlds for you to discover when it comes to tabletop roleplaying games, and you have the chance to find and define where you fit into the space. It might be hard to decide how you want to make these worlds. Do you have ideas of cities, towns, even planets to tell stories on? Do you have an idea for an adventuring party and you want to see what they dive into? Do you have a picture in your head of some supervillain who is going to be a challenge for a party to overcome, but you just know getting to watch that group try to beat the big bad would be one of the best things? Get ideas from things that you like, and make something fun for you and people around you to enjoy.

Not every idea you have will feel like it's the greatest, and not every idea you have will go the way you expected, but you should still see it through and see what fun you can make. You'll find your adventuring party—and you might find even more than one. This is the place to use your imagination, and this is the place to let your imagination run wild. In tabletop games you are really only limited by your creativity. Figure out whether you want fantasy or science fiction. Decide if you want to go to space or to go underground. You can fight hordes and armies of evil skeletons or unravel the mystery of who took the last piece of pie.

There's a game for almost every mood, and if you can't find just what you're looking for, then sometimes that's how you end up making one. You belong in this community, and you belong in these worlds. Whether you are someone making a game or someone playing a game, you belong here, and it is your chance to shine.

Never forget that you fit in the gaming community even as you get older and play new games and meet new people. Never forget that your game has value right away because you made it. You can only get better at storytelling, and as you learn more about yourself and the people you play with, you'll learn new tricks and skills to make your games even more fun! Believe in yourself, and keep creating because even if your first, second, or third idea doesn't become exactly what you want, you'll have learned so much from those stories and designs. You might not figure out your favorite kind of character, or your best voice, or the most comfortable outfits, but the process is what will make you an incredible tabletop player. Also, just have fun! It's okay to be nerdy and weird as long as you're kind and respectful. Learn from other people doing this stuff, and figure out what makes you unique.

It is your turn to roll the dice, so go ahead and roll initiative!

CHARACTER SHEET

Name _____

Age _____

Height _____

Hair color _____

Eye color _____

Favorite food _____

Favorite color _____

Four interesting facts about them:

1. _____

   _____

2. _____

   _____

3. _____

   _____

4. _____

   _____

What are they afraid of? _____

_____

How big is their family? _____

_____

What's a good memory they have? _____

_____

What sort of world do they live in? _____

_____

What are some of their goals?

    1. _____

       _____

    2. _____

       _____

    3. _____

       _____

    4. _____

       _____

5E

The most recent edition of Dungeons & Dragons, the fifth edition.

ACTUAL PLAY

A live stream or recorded session of a tabletop game for other people to enjoy. Can relate to shows like Rivals of Waterdeep, Critical Role, The Adventure Zone, and Into the Motherlands.

ADVENTURE

A set of game sessions united by characters and narrative sequence, setting, or goal.

ATTRIBUTES

Usually numbers on a character sheet that define how good a character is at a skill. They are also referred to as your character's stats (statistics). This can be things like strength, intelligence, charisma and will vary in different games.

BALANCE

Making sure a game has an equal amount of different options with mechanics, story points, or whatever pieces you let people choose from, or if they're not equal, making it intentional so that it doesn't break the game.

BIG, BAD, EVIL GAL/GUY (BBEG)

A big villain or boss that a playable character must face.

BREAK THE GAME

A mechanic, rule, or part of the game that can be misinterpreted or misused to play the game differently than intended, giving a major advantage, taking written text out of context, or otherwise.

BUG

A mechanic not working as intended or not clearly outlined so that it can be taken advantage of.

CAMPAIGN

A series of adventures.

CHARACTER SHEET

A record of a player character in a roleplaying game, including details, notes, game statistics, and background information a player would need during a play session.

COMPETITIVE PARTY GAMES

Games you play as a competition against others at the table.

CRITICAL

An extra-effective role. It may be a stronger attack, a faster move, or something else special in the game. Depending on the system this could mean rolling more dice or doubling a total when adding up all the numbers. Some criticals happen simply by rolling a natural number on a die.

CRUNCHY

A system that is rules-heavy.

DIE

The singular version of the word "dice," used to refer to a single one: "roll the six-sided die," "roll the eight-sided die." It's almost always used when you're describing something about that particular die you want the person to roll.

DIFFICULTY CLASS (DC)

A target number to save from an effect.

DUNGEON CRAWL

Navigating through a dungeon-style adventure. Not literally crawling, thankfully.

DUNGEON MASTER (DM)

Also referred to as storyteller, narrator, or game master. Primarily used for D&D.

EXPLODING DICE

In dice mechanics, when you get to roll a die again and add the results.

FUMBLE

A roll that is less effective; as an attack it might be an automatic miss, or a character might see directly through your lie. A fumble can happen simply by rolling a natural number on the die in some systems.

GAME DESIGNER

Someone who works on the design and creation of the game itself. They can be working on the story, mechanics, rules, or even the testing side of it, and they help to balance the game.

GAME MASTER (GM)

Also referred to as storyteller, narrator, or dungeon master.

HIT POINTS (HP)

Used in games to track how much health your character has.

HOMEBREW

Non-official game content created by you or others to be used in your games or experiences for a system that isn't natively built in.

INITIATIVE

The determination of who goes first and in what order declared actions are carried out.

LIVE-ACTION ROLEPLAY (LARP)

A type of interactive roleplaying game in which the participants portray characters through physical action, often in costume and with props.

MECHANICS

The rules the game follows: if this happens, then that happens. How the players interact with the game and how the game tells the story.

METAGAME

Using knowledge about the game's rules or something your character hasn't learned in the game to affect the story.

MODIFIER

Many games use modifiers to literally modify your game rolls. It may make the number higher or lower; maybe it won't affect what you roll at all. Another word for this is "bonus."

NATURAL NUMBER

The result of a die before any bonuses or adjustments are made. Some games have them as a critical or fumble depending on the result. Example, a "natural 20" may be a critical success on a d20 and a "natural 1" may be a fumble on a d20.

NON-PLAYER CHARACTER (NPC)

Any character that isn't controlled by a player of the party and is instead controlled by the game master, dungeon master, narrator, or storyteller.

OLD SCHOOL RENAISSANCE (OSR)

New TTRPGs that are inspired by the earlier editions of D&D and the games that came out in the '70s and '80s

ONE-SHOT

A game experience you can finish in one session.

OUT OF CHARACTER (OOC)

When you speak at the table as yourself, the player, instead of as your character, for example, during discussion or planning.

PLAYER CHARACTER (PC)

Any characters that are controlled by a player of the party and are not controlled by the game master, dungeon master, narrator, or storyteller.

PLAYER VS. PLAYER (PVP)

When players fight against each other.

PLAYERS VS. ENVIRONMENT (PVE)

When players fight against creatures or enemies that are controlled not by other players but by the DM or the narrator.

PLAYTESTING

The process by which a game designer tests a new game for bugs and design flaws by playing it before deciding whether it is ready to go.

RETCON

Redo and/or take back a moment in a game, often when safety tools are implemented, or when the plot changes and a player simply wants a different outcome.

ROLEPLAY

Taking on the role of a character and speaking as/for them in third or first person.

ROLL

A throw of the die or dice to achieve/determine an outcome. Rolls are how most actions or moments or events are resolved according to mechanics and rules.

RULES-HEAVY

A game system with detailed mechanics, usually providing a wide variety of possible actions in a game. The opposite of rules-lite.

RULES-LITE

A game system that uses general mechanics, usually more focused on narrative actions in a game. The opposite of rules-heavy.

SAVING THROW

A game mechanic in which dice are used to avoid a negative effect on a character.

SESSION

Playing a game together for a specified amount of time.

SESSION 0

A session before playing to establish comfort, consent, and things people do and don't want to see in their games.

STEAMPUNK

A genre of science fiction that has a historical setting and typically features steam-powered machinery rather than advanced technology.

SYSTEM

The set of game mechanics that make up a game.

SYSTEM REFERENCE DOCUMENT (SRD)

A free resource that offers guidelines for game designers to look up what's allowed to be used or published in a new game from that system.

TOKENS

Miniatures to represent specific characters or objects in a game.

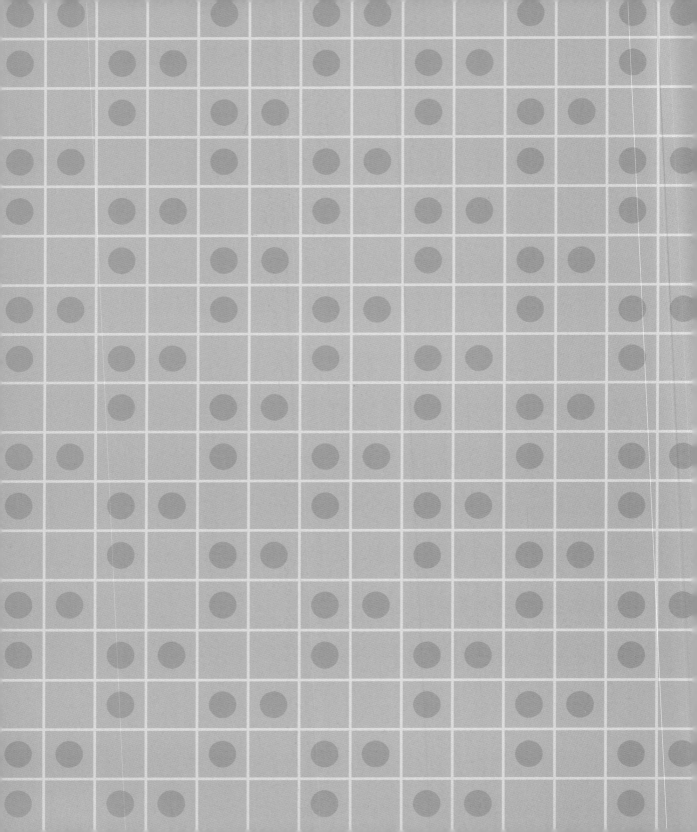

DIGITAL WEBSITES FOR TABLETOP GAMES

Speak to an older family member and ask them to help you
get set up using some of these online resources and to find games!

D&D BEYOND

D&D Beyond is the official digital tool set and game companion for Dungeons & Dragons, fifth edition. DDB hosts online versions of the official Dungeons & Dragons 5e books, including rule books.

DRIVE THRU RPG

Drive Thru RPG is a digital marketplace company for both major and indie games and currently the largest RPG download store to purchase PDFs or physical books for tabletop RPGs.

ITCH.IO

Itch.io is a website for users to host, sell, and download indie games. Creators sell PDFs of their work here for people to download and play, as well as rules or cards to print out.

ROLL20

Roll20 is a website consisting of a set of tools for playing tabletop roleplaying games, also referred to as a virtual tabletop, which can be used as an aid to playing in person or to play remotely online.

RECOMMENDED GAMES FOR KIDS

· ·

A quick list of games that are perfect for you to play to get
a feel for TTRPGs with your friends, family, or community.

· ·

AMAZING TALES

A story-making game of roleplay and imagination with rules to guide players and narrators on how to tell stories together, rolling dice to add drama and excitement for everyone.

HERO KIDS

An ENNIE award–winning fantasy RPG for kids aged four to ten. This game offers a fast and fun introduction to RPGs, perfect for younger kids who are just getting interested in roleplaying games.

KIDS ON BIKES

Stranger Things meets TTRPGs with this game where you and your party play as kids solving mysteries and grappling with strange, dangerous, and powerful forces in your small town. A great way to explore more collaborative storytelling RPGs, it comes with additional decks, books, and materials to help grow your game—plus, a whole range of spin-off series like Kids on Brooms and Teens in Space.

MY LITTLE PONY: TAILS OF EQUESTRIA

Inspired by the popular world of *My Little Pony*, this storytelling game allows you and your party to explore the amazing and magical world of Equestria. Will you be a dynamic adventurer like Daring Do or a stylish diva like Rarity? Tails of Equestria allows you to create,

name, and play as your very own pony character to solve puzzles and explore dungeons—
and there may even be some dragons!

QUESTLINGS

A TTRPG where players play as two characters: one is your kid form, and one is your Inner
Hero! The game guides players and GMs using a map accompanied with a storybook as a
framework for roleplaying and building the story.

WITCHCRAFT: MAGIC OF HEREVA

Based on the ongoing webcomic *Pepper and Carrot*, this charming fantasy game takes place
in the world of Hereva, where everyone and everything can do at least a little magic. It has
a great balance of magic and adventure, perfect for any group.

Acknowledgments

Tabletop RPGs are my passion and my job. They've given me a space to take the creativity I was so afraid to share as a kid and make something amazing out of it. I remember over and over wondering whether I would be able to make good stories when I was younger, and I wish I'd had this book to see all the stuff I could do. Shout-out to all of those who let me interview them, because they're not only peers but also people who have inspired me and I knew would make a difference. A huge acknowledgment to my mentor, Luke Peterschmidt, who always told me to pursue anything I was passionate about and helped me prove to myself that I could genuinely make it work in this world if I get working for it.

ABOUT
THE AUTHOR

GABE HICKS is a nerd in many ways. He has worked on projects for Pathfinder, Starfinder, Critical Role, The Adventure Zone, and plenty of other big names in the gaming business. He doesn't have a favorite tabletop RPG system, but he loves to make his own new ones, even if they only get played once. He has spent time as a creative producer at Roll20 and occasionally freelances as a narrator for one-shot adventures. He has no idea what the next big adventure will be, but he always says, "I'm incredibly excited to see it, and I'm even more excited for the loot."

ABOUT
THE ILLUSTRATOR

DAVE PERILLO is an illustrator and designer based out of the Philadelphia suburbs. With the help of an Ed Emberly drawing book, hours of cartoons, and a "healthy" diet of sugary cereals, he doodled his way through school and on to college to study graphic design. His first position was as an illustrator in the glamorous world of medical publishing. After countless drawings of dancing kidneys and otoscopes, he felt a need to feed his creative juices and began to create his own pop culture–inspired art. This path launched him into a world of comic conventions, art galleries, and freelance design. He developed his retro art style and use of a limited color palette from his love of the mid-century modern aesthetic. Dave has done work for many prestigious clients including Disney, Marvel, Target, Lucasfilm, Pixar, Nickelodeon, and Cartoon Network, to name a few. To see more of Dave's work, check out www.daveperilloart.com.

IT IS DANGEROUS TO GO ALONE, HERE TAKE THIS!

A KID'S GUIDE TO FANDOM

EXPLORING FAN-FIC, COSPLAY, GAMING, PODCASTING, AND MORE IN THE GEEK WORLD!

Written by AMY RATCLIFFE
Illustrated by DAVE PERILLO